STORAGE
SOLUTIONS

Create a home for everything with
these practical storage ideas

STORAGE
SOLUTIONS

p

This is a Parragon Book
First printed in 2002

Parragon
Queen Street House
4 Queen Street
Bath BA1 1HE
United Kingdom

Created and produced by The Bridgewater Book Company Ltd, Lewes, East Sussex

Art Directors Colin Fielder, Sarah Howerd, Michael Whitehead
Editorial Director Fiona Biggs
Editor Sarah Yelling
Photographers Steve Gorton, Alistair Hughes, Steve Tanner

ISBN: 0-75256-993-7

Printed in China

Contents

Introduction

The word 'decluttering' is very much part of our vocabulary in this new millennium. There are whole shops devoted to it, and you can actually pay a consultant by the hour to come round to your house and advise you on how to declutter your belongings and put everything away in the correct place. This book, however, shows you how to 'declutter' your home yourself – quickly, easily, stylishly and cheaply – with a selection of practical storage projects that will make tidying up a positive joy at the end of the day. Every room in the house is covered in detail.

ABOVE **Hanging a rail beneath the shelves in a small kitchen will free up a huge amount of cupboard space. Display matching sets of plain-coloured crockery for a cool contemporary look, or mismatching flowered or striped tea cups for that country cottage feel.**

The kitchen is a room that people often 'live with', because ripping all the units out and starting again can be very expensive, not to mention disruptive. Developments in DIY practices, however, mean that more primers and paint finishes are available than ever before, which means you don't have to live with those beige melamine cupboards! The projects in the Cabinet Makeovers section show you how to change the doors on kitchen units, replace them with slide-out wicker baskets, or even paint them in a zingy colour. Nothing is impossible – and you don't have to even think about buying a new kitchen.

Shelves are about as far as some people go on the do-it-yourself front, but even these humble items can be made to look funky and interesting. If you have a yen for a cool modern interior, why not go for the floating shelves? These are simplicity itself to put up and look quite amazing, especially when accessorised with ice-blue walls and silver accessories. Or, if you fancy something a little more traditional, try the adjustable room-height shelving, which can be adapted to any room size. These shelves can all be painted and stained to match your colour scheme.

As more and more people choose to work from home, it is becomingly increasingly necessary for a greater divide to exist between home-life clutter and office clutter. The projects detailed here make this easy.

Whether you have a whole room devoted to your work, or just a small understairs space, a portable desk-top unit and a storage unit on castors will prove to be invaluable pieces of equipment. The stylish curved desk will fit into most room schemes, and can be painted in whatever colour you like. It is also extremely easy to construct.

So, what are you waiting for? Being neat has never been easier! Take a look round your home, decide what it needs, then pick a project and get making, sewing or constructing. In this beautifully and clearly photographed book, there are storage solutions to every problem.

ABOVE **An attractive fabric-covered screen will hide television and video equipment in your living room. Use traditional damask or tapestry fabric for a cosy, old-fashioned look, or try fake animal furs and skins for a more modern feel.**

LEFT **A shower caddy quickly becomes indispensable and you'll wonder how you managed without one. Your bathroom will become much tidier too!**

On The Shelf

Shelves are an indispensable piece of furniture
in any room of the house and, because they quickly become colonised with
books, plants and ornaments, it is wise to put up a good selection. Shelves are
also immensely versatile and can be made to fit into any room style and made
to match any colour scheme. The projects on the following pages describe a
variety of useful shelving solutions, from the ultra-modern floating shelf to
the softer idea of fabric hanging shelves. There is also a handy shelf unit for
the shower, and fabric screens which are used to actually conceal
understairs shelves and storage areas.

PROJECT ONE

Adjustable room-height shelving

You can customise your shelving to suit your individual household requirements with this entirely versatile scheme. Constructed simply from the same wood stock, it can form part of a cladding project, or be fixed directly to a decorated wall surface. Any varnished timber finish can be used to match a room scheme.

If planned and measured accurately, different batten grids fixed to a wall can serve as a secure base for a variety of projects. Using this grid, a shelving system can run at right angles to the vertical cladding and can perform functional or decorative duties. An advantage is that all wood stock is the same size, 50 x 25mm/2 x 1in, so you can buy in bulk from a wood merchant. The system has been devised to support 127mm/5in-wide shelves, but, if this is too wide, it can easily be revised to accept 100-mm/4-in shelves that will still hold paperbacks and decorative objects. Simply cut

the slot-in shelf supports to 100mm/4in rather than 127mm/5in. Any number of shelf uprights can be incorporated into this versatile scheme, depending on the length of the shelves that will complete the wall. Reckon on one support for every seven TGV uprights, if using 90-mm/3½-in cladding, which gives a support every 630mm/25in. Aim to space out and fix the wall battens. Plug the wall even if you have bare brick, because of the weight the uprights might have to take. Use number 8 countersunk 50-mm/2-in steel screws, butting short horizontal lengths between the floor to the ceiling shelf-support battens. All battens should be 50 x 25mm/2 x 1in.

Shelving supports

This system employs two sizes of vertical support, screwed to the face of the wall support, creating a gap, into which the horizontal pieces that will support the shelf are slotted. For each upright you will need wood pieces cut from the same stock 127mm/5in long, positioned starting from flush top, leaving 18-mm/¾-in dividing gaps as you progress down the length. These pieces are secured by centre drilling 38mm/1½in from the bottom edge, and screwing through to the upright using 32-mm/1¼-in number 8 – raised – countersunk head brass screws and seatings. This gives a screw finish resembling a brass stud. A second layer of support pieces is needed only where the shelf supports are to be slotted in. 76-mm/3-in pieces are thus screwed flush with the top of the designated

This versatile adjustable shelving system can be installed on its own or as part of a wall cladding system. It is constructed from simple 50 x 25mm/2 x 1in softwood battens. It can be painted or stained in your chosen colours.

127-mm/5-in pieces by centre drilling 38mm/1½in from the bottom edge in exactly the same way as before. Slot in the shelf support horizontals, which are also 127-mm/5-in pieces, to check the fit in the slot and to see if they hold a spirit-levelled shelf correctly. When you are happy with everything, sand all the pieces lightly to remove sharp edges and any splinters. For added strength, you can glue as well as screw the pieces together.

Finishing the wall

Now that the shelving system is complete, invisibly pin the TGV uprights to the horizontal battens. Seven should fit snugly between the uprights. Plane the wood to fit the wall edges. The join at the TGV can be expanded slightly to take up a minor shortfall. The cladding can be varnished, as can the shelving uprights and support pieces, and a skirting added. Finally the shelf supports can be slotted into place.

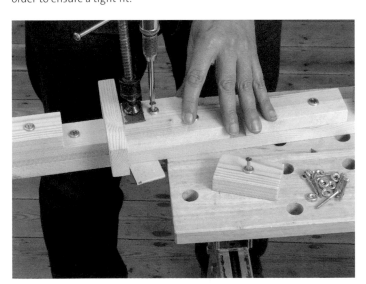

STEP 1 Lay out the 127mm/5in-long pieces of timber on the wall support batten. It is advisable to space them with the shelf battens in order to ensure a tight fit.

STEP 2 The next stage is to cramp and then screw the sections of timber to the support batten. For this you should use countersunk-head brass screws and screw seats.

STEP 3 Attach the 76-mm/3-in lengths of batten to the first lengths in the same manner, flush with the top edge. You should use countersunk-head brass screws and seats as before.

STEP 4 Finally, check the fit of the shelf support battens in their slots. It is important that the fit is exact; if the shelf supports are loose, the shelf will not be stable.

YOU WILL NEED:
- **FLOATING SHELF PACK – INCLUDING SPECIAL FITTINGS, SCREWS AND WALL PLUGS (AVAILABLE IN DIY STORES)**
- **TAPE MEASURE/ LONG RULER**
- **STRAIGHT EDGE WITH BUILT-IN SPIRIT LEVEL**
- **PENCIL**
- **DRILL**
- **CORRECT DRILL BIT FOR YOUR WALL, I.E. MASONRY OR PLASTERBOARD**

PROJECT TWO

Floating shelves

The essence of the cool, minimalist style is that rooms should appear to be emptier than they actually are. Create the impression of open space by fitting shelving that seems to float in the air without any visible support system. There are several different systems on the market that work very efficiently, so instead of 're-inventing the wheel' the project shows how to use one of the existing designs. Choose a length to suit the proportions of your walls and the things you wish to display, as it is important to keep to the open uncluttered style.

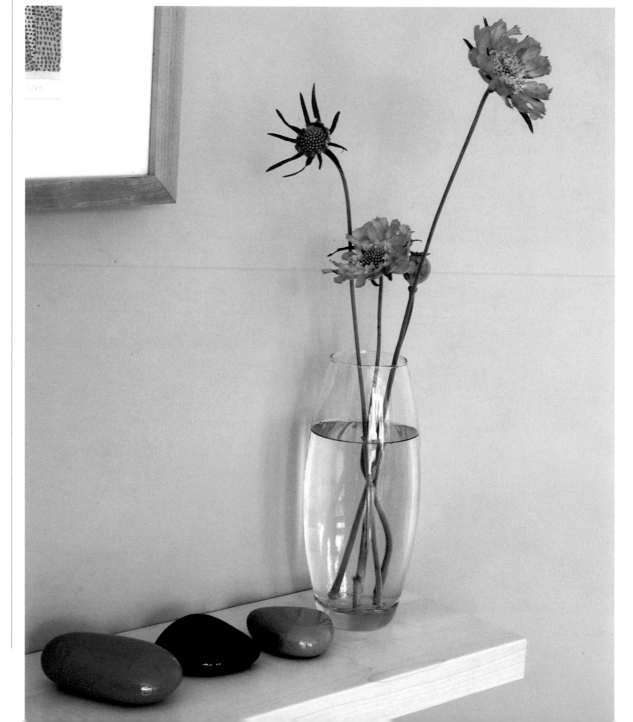

These simple shelves seem to float in space. They blend in well with a minimalist decorating scheme.

HOW TO DO IT

Simple to fit and a minimalist's dream, these shelves are magical. But, as with most tricks, the explanation is quite simple.

STEP 1 Having decided on the best position for the shelf, measure and mark it on the wall lightly in pencil.

STEP 2 Hold the support up to the wall and check it with the spirit level.

STEP 3 Mark the fixing positions for the supports then remove them and drill and plug the wall.

STEP 4 Fix the shelf onto the wall supports.

YOU WILL NEED:

- WOODEN BATTEN,
  12MM/$\frac{1}{2}$IN THICK,
  25MM/1IN WIDE
- SEW-ON TOUCH-AND-CLOSE TAPE
- STAPLE GUN
- TAPE MEASURE
- LENGTH OF
  PATTERNED FABRIC
- LENGTH OF
  PLAIN FABRIC
- NEEDLE AND THREAD
- SEWING MACHINE
- METAL EYELETS
- EYELET PLIERS
- AIR-ERASABLE PEN
- CUP HOOKS
- PINS
- SCISSORS
- STEAM IRON

PROJECT THREE
Shelving hideaways

Most of us have areas in the home that would benefit from being kept hidden – an alcove of dishevelled books or a bathroom shelving unit full of mismatched toiletries.

Luckily these can be concealed from view behind fabric blinds or screens. A Roman or roller blind is great for hiding all sorts of clutter, and you can just draw it up for access.

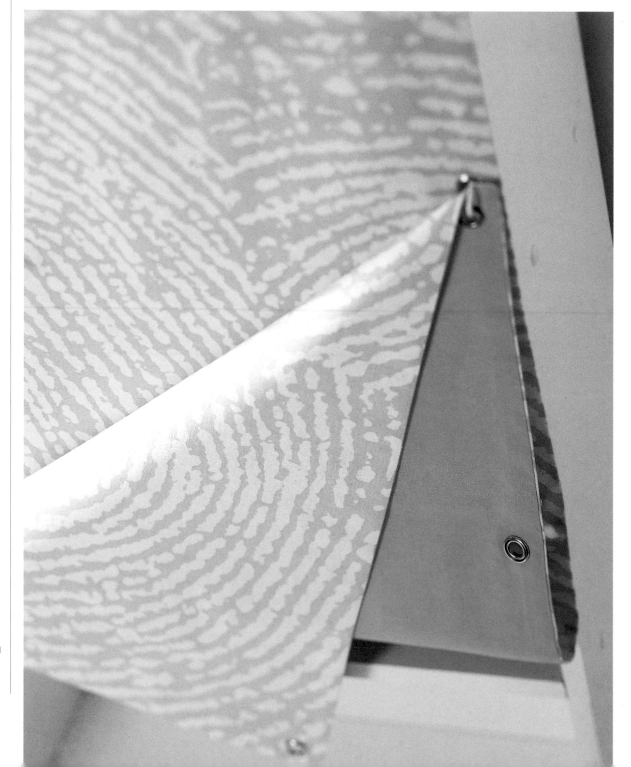

Shelving hideaways can be used to conceal a multitude of things. Use fabric that holds its shape well.

HOW TO DO IT

Make this smart cover to hang in front of an open cupboard, alcove or shelving unit. The cover is hung from a wooden batten fixed to the upper edge, and a row of eyelets along the side edges is slipped onto hooks so the cover can be held open at different levels. The cover has a contrast lining, so it is reversible to ring the changes and can be hooked open to reveal the underside.

STEP 1 Fix a 12mm/¹/₂in-thick, 25mm/1in-wide wooden batten to the upper edge of the open area. It should extend at least 25mm/1in on each side of the open area. Staple the stiff section of sew-on touch-and-close tape to the batten. Measure the length of the batten and the drop of the cover from the top of the batten. For the cover, cut one rectangle or square of the main fabric and one of contrast fabric that is the length of the batten plus 32mm/1¹/₄in by the drop plus 32mm/1¹/₄in.

STEP 2 With the right sides facing, stitch the covers together, taking a 15-mm/⁵/₈-in seam allowance and leaving a gap to turn on the upper edge. Clip the corners, turn right side out and press.

STEP 3 Tack and stitch the corresponding length of touch-and-close tape to the upper edge of the cover.

STEP 4 Following the manufacturer's instructions, fix a 15-mm/⁵/₈-in diameter metal eyelet 20mm/³/₄in within the lower corners. Use an air-erasable pen to mark eyelet positions 20mm/³/₄in within the side edges approximately 230mm/9in apart. Fix the eyelets in place with the eyelet pliers. Press the cover onto the batten. Fix cup hooks to the wall or wood surround under each eyelet.

YOU WILL NEED:

- VARIOUS
  ABRASIVE PAPERS
- SANDING BLOCK
- SCREWDRIVER
- WHITE LIMING WAX
- CLEAR WAX
- COLOURED
  PIGMENTS
- FINE STEEL WOOL
- POLISHING CLOTH
- WOOD GLUE

PROJECT FOUR

Kitchen shelves

An old self-assembly pine unit that had fallen apart and been thrown in a skip provided a perfect set of surfaces for subtle waxed finishes, each one looking as if it were reflecting a different coloured light into the room – a great improvement on the original finish.

STEP 1 The unit was loosely re-assembled, and the original surface removed using medium grade, followed by fine grade, wet silicon carbide abrasive paper.

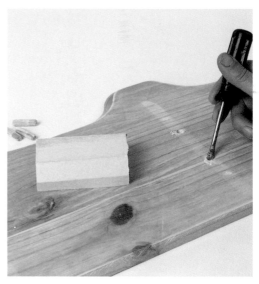

STEP 2 The finish residue was removed from the dowel holes using an old screwdriver, and the surface sanded using 240 grit aluminium oxide around a sanding block.

STEP 3 Clear wax mixed with colour pigment was rubbed into the grain with fine steel wool.

STEP 4 The waxed surfaces were polished to a fine sheen using a soft, lint-free cloth.

STEP 5 Wood glue was run into the dowel holes, prior to re-insertion of the fluted dowels.

STEP 6 Re-assembly – the colour-waxed shelves were glued to the other half of the dowels.

YOU WILL NEED:

• CLOSELY WOVEN
  FABRIC – SUCH AS
  CALICO, DENIM
  OR CANVAS
• NEEDLE AND THREAD
• SEWING MACHINE
• TAILOR'S CHALK
• LONG RULER
• PINS
• CORRUGATED
  CARDBOARD
• SEW-ON
  TOUCH-AND-CLOSE
  TAPE
• SCISSORS
• STEAM IRON
• 3 METAL PAPER
  FASTENERS

PROJECT FIVE

Hanging shelves

A set of sturdy fabric hanging shelves is great for storing T-shirts and knitwear. The shelves are applied to a wardrobe rail with a hanging strap that fastens with touch-and-close tape. The shelves are reinforced with corrugated card and are very lightweight.

Use a colourful striped canvas to make this useful set of hanging shelves. Remember to position the stripes centrally when cutting out the fabric pieces.

HOW TO DO IT

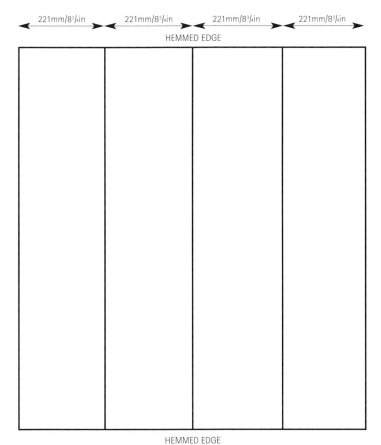

221mm/8³⁄₄in 221mm/8³⁄₄in 221mm/8³⁄₄in 221mm/8³⁄₄in

HEMMED EDGE

HEMMED EDGE

Use this diagram to
cut out the fabric for
the hanging shelves.
Draw lines in tailor's
chalk as indicated to
divide the piece of fabric
into four equal sections.

STEP 1 Refer to the diagram to cut a
rectangle of fabric for the support 980 x
885mm/3ft 2³⁄₄in x 2ft 10³⁄₄in. Press 10mm/³⁄₈in
under then 15mm/⁵⁄₈in on the short edges.
Stitch close to the inner pressed edges.

STEP 2 Cut three shelves from fabric
623 x 310mm/24¹⁄₂ x 12¹⁄₄in. With the wrong sides
facing, press the shelves widthways in half and
topstitch 6mm/¹⁄₄in from the pressed edges;
these will be the front edges. Pin the opposite
raw edges together; these will be at the back
of the shelves.

STEP 3 Draw the lines on the wrong side
of the support using tailor's chalk. With the
underside of the shelves facing the support,
pin the back edge of the shelves along the lines,
matching the centres.

STEP 4 Tack the shelves in place. Cut five 275-mm/10¾-in squares of corrugated cardboard. Slip one square centrally inside the middle shelf. Pin the raw edges together to enclose the card.

STEP 5 Fold the support around each side of the middle shelf, matching the raw edges to the drawn lines. Pin and tack the side edges of the shelves to the support. Insert a square of cardboard into the remaining shelves, and pin and tack them to the support in the same way.

STEP 6 Fold the support along the lines at the back of the shelves, enclosing the raw shelf edges. Pin and stitch the back edge taking a 6-mm/¼-in seam allowance, and starting and finishing 6mm/¼in from the side edges of the shelves. Fold the support along the lines at the sides of the shelves, enclosing the raw shelf edges. Pin and stitch the side edges, taking a 6-mm/¼-in seam allowance, starting at the back seam and continuing to the front hemmed edges.

STEP 7 Cut a rectangle of fabric for the hanging strap 293 x 200mm/ 11½ x 8in. Press 6mm/¼in under then 10mm/⅜in on the short edges. Stitch close to the inner edges. Press 10mm/⅜in under on one long edge. Pin and stitch one section of sew-on touch-and-close tape on top. Press 10mm/⅜in under on the right side on the other long edge. Pin and stitch the other section of touch-and-close tape on top.

STEP 8 Cut two rectangles of fabric 642 x 330mm/2ft 1¼in x 13in for the roof and base. Mark widthways across the centre of the roof with pins. Pin the hanging strap centrally to one half of the roof, with the right sides facing and the long edges of the strap parallel to the centre line. Stitch the strap to the roof 12mm /½in each side of the centre of the strap. Remove the pins.

STEP 9 With the right sides facing, fold the roof and base widthways in half. Stitch the short edges, taking a 10-mm/⅜-in seam allowance. Clip the corners, turn right side out and press. Topstitch 6mm/¼in from the pressed edges; these will be the front edges. Slip a cardboard square inside. Secure the roof layers together with three metal paper fasteners along the centre of the strap. With the top of the roof facing the right side of the back of the support, stitch the roof centrally to the upper edge, taking a 10-mm/⅜-in seam allowance. Stitch the base to the lower edge in the same way. Clip the seam allowance diagonally at the end of the seam on the roof and base .

STEP 10 Press 10mm/⅜in under on the raw edges of the support. Fold the roof and base over the seams. Stitch the back edge 8mm/ ⁵⁄₁₆in from the seam, starting and finishing 8mm/⁵⁄₁₆in inside the side edges. Pin the pressed edges and sides of the roof together. Stitch close to the outer edges. Stitch 6mm/ ¼in inside the edges, starting 8mm/⁵⁄₁₆in from the back edge. Repeat for the base.

PROJECT SIX

Shower caddy

Trying to locate the soap, shampoo or sponge can be highly frustrating when water is cascading into your eyes. This simple solution should help to keep everything you need in one place, close to hand when you need it. It is ideally suited to a tiled wall and its beauty lies in the fact that only two holes are drilled through the tiling, with the rest going into the wooden support.

This shower caddy lets you have a range of fittings with only two holes drilled through the tiles. All the rest are drilled to the wooden caddy.

HOW TO DO IT

STEP 1 Find the ideal position for the caddy on the shower wall, making quite sure that there are no pipes behind the tiles where the screws will be located! Mark the positions for the components and the shelf.

STEP 2 Drill two evenly spaced holes in the shelf end.

STEP 3 Screw the top shelf to the back plank using brass cupped screws. Screw the coat hook and soap dish into position.

STEP 4 Place the unit in position on the wall. Mark through the pre-drilled holes onto the wall using a bradawl.

STEP 5 Drill holes through the tiles using the masking tape to stop the tile bit from skidding. Plug the wall.

STEP 6 Screw the unit to the wall using the brass cupped screws.

PROJECT SEVEN
Storage box sections

Whether you need to reinforce sagging shelves with vertical supports or make up a self-supporting unit with stepped sides, the same simple wood joint can be used. Halving joints allow the shelves to slot together at right angles, forming an unseen bond which can also be used as a decorative feature.

Weight for support

Shelving systems, constructed from 25-mm/1-in boards or 18-mm/¾-in plywood machined to size, are ideal for fixing in an alcove. The recess will generally be less than 1.8m/6ft wide and the shelf length, if supported on battens to the side and rear, will be perfectly stable. Longer lengths, needed to span a gap where, say, two rooms have been knocked into one and the resultant distance between chimney breasts is over 3m/10ft, are liable to sag, particularly if they are 300mm/12in in width.

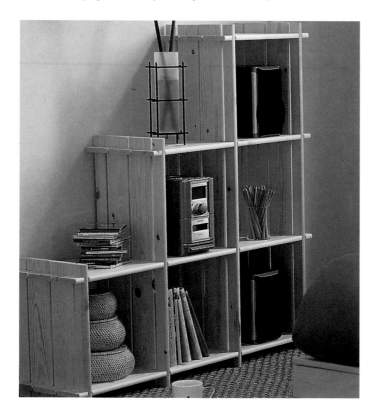

A modular box-section storage system can provide a versatile means of containing and displaying a wide variety of domestic objects. Such systems can be tailored to meet your specific needs.

Front support pieces, glued and screwed under and flush with the front edge of each shelf, will help, but heavy weights will still cause problems.

It is reasonable to assume that a long, wide shelf will be used to hold larger, heavier items than a small shelf, so it must be constructed with more support. Loadbearing shelves can have brackets screwed underneath, either as separate fixed items or as part of an adjustable shelving system, where removable brackets are slotted into steel uprights screwed to the wall. There are numerous adjustable systems on the market, all using the same principle, and the heavy-duty ones are very strong indeed. The wall fixings must involve no less than 56-mm/2¼-in number 10 countersunk screws driven into heavy-duty wall plugs. The uprights should be spaced 750mm/2½ft apart. Heavy-duty adjustable shelving is available in only very basic colours, however. Although you can paint it yourself, and it may look effective in a workroom, garage or outbuilding, it isn't exactly subtle. There is a better, much more attractive loadbearing support system for a living area, which you can construct yourself.

A self-supporting box system

This is a simple wooden unit that relies on horizontal and vertical boards meeting at a series of halving joints and providing mutual support. A halving joint is simple to cut and, when accurate, extremely strong and virtually invisible. The principle behind halving joints (also called half-and-half joints or half-laps) is that where the timbers meet or overlap at right-angles, one exact half of each timber is cut and removed to allow the pieces to slot

STEP 1 Cut the first half of the joint in one board. You can subsequently use it as a template to mark the matching half with your marking knife.

STEP 2 Cut the joint by making a series of saw cuts through the waste to the bottom of each of the slots. Then remove the waste with a thin chisel.

STEP 3 Then check the fit of each of the joints. They should all be snug, and making saw cuts on the waste side of each marked line should ensure this.

STEP 4 Glue inside the housings of the corresponding joint halves and carefully assemble the boards.

STEP 5 Cramp and wipe off glue. The unit can be strengthened by gluing and pinning on a plywood backing.

together. The timbers can be cramped securely, marked out with a knife and cut together so that the housings are the same width as the thickness of the wood, and cut back with a chisel to a shoulder half the width of the timber. Always saw on the waste side of the marked line when cutting halving joints. If you don't, the housings will be too wide by the width of the saw blade, and the joint will be loose.

Custom building

Any size of unit can be constructed in this way, depending on your storage requirements, and the space available. A drawing dividing the wall space into compartments is a good start. These can be any size, but square is easy and uniformly attractive. Consider using measurements that turn the unit into a series of cubes: if your chosen timber is 300mm/1ft-wide, use the same figure for the internal dimensions of each box. A scaled-down model made of card will give you a better idea of how it will look – slots cut in the card will join together in exactly the same way as the timbers. The top of the unit need not reach the ceiling. A long top shelf for houseplants and ornaments is created by forming external corners, which are simply one-sided halving joints. Your unit is floor-standing, so you need to consider a plinth for the base, and this should be the height of the skirting. Flush at the front and sides, the plinth can be set forward the width of the skirting at the back of the base, so that the unit back is flush with the wall.

Securing and backing

If you are making a small unit, cramping it square as you glue the joints will ensure it is stable enough. Larger units can be glued in sections as you proceed, but any 'play' in the halving joints will result in undue pressure being placed on the unit's square corners. A support batten glued and screwed under the top back edge of each top corner box will hold that corner square, and allow you to drill through and fix the unit to the wall. If you prefer, you can attach a back panel, placing the unit face-down, and confirming that it is square.

Cut 6-mm/¼-in plywood to fit the outside back, and glue and pin into position with panel pins. Make sure that the best side of the plywood is visible from the front. The unit is now stable and free-standing. Screws driven through the backing into the wall can be used to provide extra security, if this is required.

Hang-Ups

Hanging things up and out of the way can minimise
clutter amazingly, and make for a much tidier home. A smart peg rail, for
example, makes sure that coats and hats have a permanent home all year round,
while a slick chrome rod in the kitchen gets utensils out and within easy reach,
freeing up vital drawer space. A shelf above a rail is particularly useful in
a child's bedroom; toys can be stored on the shelf, while bags of bricks and
figures can hang neatly from the pegs below. A softwood pinboard is a fun
accessory in teenagers' rooms, allowing them to stick up those
essential phone numbers and study lists.

YOU WILL NEED:
- 50 x 25-mm/ 2 x 1-in PAR TIMBER, THE LENGTH OF YOUR WALL
- WOODEN PEGS OR 2m/6FT OF 25-MM DOWEL
- 25-MM/1-IN SPADE BIT
- DRILL
- MEDIUM GRADE SANDPAPER
- WOOD GLUE
- STRAIGHT EDGE WITH BUILT-IN SPIRIT LEVEL
- TAPE MEASURE
- PENCIL
- WALL PLUGS
- NO. 6 MASONRY AND A COUNTERSINK BIT AND A 6-MM CLEARANCE BIT
- 32-MM/1¼-IN No. 8 COUNTERSINK SCREWS FOR FIXINGS
- WOOD FILLER
- PRIMER
- SHAKER BLUE PAINT
- PAINTBRUSH

PROJECT ONE
A Shaker-style peg rail

The Shakers were a religious group who lived communally. They needed plenty of clear floor space for their meetings so they hung their chairs from rails on the wall. The Shakers are famous for their simple but beautifully crafted furniture, much of which was 'built in' to keep the rooms plain-looking, although they found ways of adding decorative touches without breaking the religion's strict guidelines on ornament. Shaker style has become very popular in the past decade and fits in very well with the modern trend for decluttering.

A brightly coloured peg rail is useful in any room of the house. Children's rooms will benefit the most from an arrangement like this one.

HOW TO DO IT

Peg rails can be positioned at the most useful height for any room – up high in the bathroom or low down in a child's bedroom.

STEP 1 Cut the timber lengths to fit. Mark the positions for the fixings (one screw per metre of rail). Drill out the holes and mark the positions on the wall roughly 1.5m/4ft from the floor. Drill and plug the holes.

STEP 2 Mark out the positions for the pegs along the rail. They should not be too close together; consider the room's proportions and allow a spacing of 300mm–500mm/12in–20in. Fit the spade bit to the drill and make the holes for the pegs (at an angle of 45°).

STEP 3 If using dowel, cut it into 100-mm/4-in lengths for the pegs. Smooth the exposed ends to a neat rounded finish and rub the sides of the 'sinking' ends on the sandpaper to slim them slightly so that they fit snugly into the drilled holes.

STEP 4 Squeeze wood glue into the holes and coat the sinking ends of the pegs. Tap them in position, then wipe away any excess glue. Leave to set. Paint the pegs and the rail in your chosen colour.

STEP 5 Finally, screw the peg rail onto the wall, then cover the screw-heads with wood filler and touch up with paint once it has dried.

YOU WILL NEED:
- STEEL OR CHROME RAIL WITH HOOKS (OR TWO CHROME TOWEL RAIL HOLDERS AND A LENGTH OF RAIL)
- STRAIGHT EDGE WITH A BUILT-IN SPIRIT LEVEL
- MASKING TAPE IF THE WALL IS TILED
- DRILL
- CORRECT SIZE MASONRY DRILL BIT FOR THE SCREWS (E.G. SCREW SIZE No. 6, BIT SIZE No. 6)
- WALL PLUGS

PROJECT TWO

Fitting a chrome utensil rail to the wall

The first thing you need to discover is what your wall is made of. The usual suspects are painted or tiled brick or plasterboard, and they require different wall fixings. There is also a knack to drilling holes in tiles successfully. Use a small strip of masking tape which has to be placed on the tile before you mark the screw position. The tape stops the drill bit from skidding off as it spins. Whether you buy a ready-made rail or make one yourself by customising a chrome towel rail, the actual task of fitting it to the wall will be the same.

Chrome utensil rails can be bought ready-made or you can make them by customising a chrome towel rail. When you are deciding which height to fit it, hang the longest utensil from the rail to make sure it's high enough.

HOW TO DO IT

STEP 1 Decide where you would like the rail on the wall and mark the position in pencil. Hold up the rail to the wall with the spirit level. Make certain that the rail is level, then accurately mark the positions for the screws.

STEP 2 Drill the holes for the wall plugs. Hold the drill at a right angle to the wall and apply firm pressure as you drill.

TIPS
• Chrome rails can be clamped to a workbench or a table edge, and cut down to size with a hacksaw.
• Wooden dowelling rods can be used with chrome towel rail fittings to give a softer look. They are especially suitable if you have wooden floors or cupboard doors.
• Buy butcher-style hooks, without sharp points, from kitchenware shops.

STEP 3 Push the plugs into the holes, tapping them lightly with a hammer if necessary. They should fit snugly and stay in place. If the hole is too big you may need to go up a size with both wall plugs and screws.

STEP 4 Screw in the top screw on each side to support the rail as you tighten the other screws.

YOU WILL NEED:
- COPPER RAIL
  AND HOOKS
- DRILL
- 2-MM/¹/₈-IN BIT FOR
  PILOT HOLES
- 40-MM/1¹/₂-IN
  NO. 8 SCREWS TO
  HOLD THE SUPPORTS
  TO THE SHELF
- SCREWDRIVER
- MITRE BLOCK
- TENON SAW
- 300MM/12IN OF
  50 x 50-MM/
  2 x 2-IN TIMBER
  FOR SUPPORTS
- 22-MM/⁷/₈-IN
  SPADE BIT

PROJECT THREE
Fitting a rail below a floating shelf

Shelves with internal brackets give the kitchen a contemporary edge, and by fitting steel rails for cups below the shelf you can double its usefulness. If you are displaying glasses, cups or mugs in this way invest in a brand new matching set so that you can enjoy looking at them. Buy the shelves from a DIY store: they will have full fitting instructions and the fixings needed to complete the job. The design of the steel rail is best kept simple – as a rule the cheaper they are the more elaborate – so shop around for a rail that pleases the eye. Some of them can be bought complete with hooks, if not, buy blunt 'S' hooks rather than authentic butcher's hooks, which have lethal points.

Open shelves fitted with steel rails provide useful storage space without blocking out areas of the galley kitchen. Matching sets of crockery are preferable to odd sets, if you are putting them on display in a contemporary kitchen.

HOW TO DO IT

STEP 1 Use the tenon saw and mitre block to cut the supports for the rail.

STEP 2 Use the 22-mm/⅞-in spade bit to drill holes in the supports to take the rail. Drill to 15-mm/⅝-in depth.

STEP 3 Drill a 4-mm clearance hole through the shelf. Countersink for the screw head. Drill the pilot hole into the bracket for the screw.

STEP 4 Fit the pipe into the hole of the fixed support and then fit the second support at the other end of the shelf. Screw this in position from above.

YOU WILL NEED:

- 75 x 25-MM/3 x 1-IN PAR SOFTWOOD TO FIT AROUND THE ROOM (MEASURE THE LENGTH REQUIRED)
- SHELF (THE SAME AMOUNT OF PAR SOFTWOOD AGAIN)
- SUPPORT BRACKETS FOR SHELF TO MATCH 75MM/3IN DEPTH OF SHELF
- PEGS (EITHER BUY TURNED PEGS OR MAKE THEM FROM A LENGTH OF DOWEL. DECIDE HOW MANY YOU NEED FOR NOW, MORE CAN ALWAYS BE ADDED LATER)
- STRAIGHT EDGE WITH BUILT-IN SPIRIT LEVEL
- PENCIL
- DRILL
- 8-MM/⁵⁄₁₆-IN BIT FOR CLEARANCE HOLES
- 6-MM/¹⁄₄-IN BIT FOR WALL FIXINGS
- SPADE BIT FOR PEGS
- 6-MM WALL PLUGS SUITABLE FOR YOUR KIND OF WALL
- 2-MM/¹⁄₁₆-IN BIT FOR PILOT HOLES

PROJECT FOUR

Fitting a peg rail and shelf

This could be a continuation of some tongue-and-groove panelling, which always looks brilliant in kid's playrooms, or a project on its own. If you decide against panelling, you may not want to fit the peg rail and shelf on more than one wall. The instructions allow for this, and explain the order and technique rather than giving exact measurements so it can be adapted.

A row of pegs can make clearing up fun. Hang a row of brightly coloured bags on the pegs to put small toys like bricks, cars or marbles in, or hang the toys directly on the pegs themselves. The shelf above offers even more storage space.

HOW TO DO IT

STEP 1 Cut the peg rail plank to fit the wall lengths, mitring the ends for a neat fit in the corners and at any joins. Check and mark the rail position on the wall with a spirit level.

STEP 2 Use the spade bit to drill holes for the pegs and then apply wood glue to their ends before pushing them firmly into the rail. If the pegs are to be painted different colours, it may be easier to do this before you fit them.

STEP 3 Drill clearance holes in the planks then mark, drill and plug the wall or wall batten, and screw the peg rail in place.

STEP 4 Screw the shelf to the peg rail or through into the wall batten. Prime and paint.

PROJECT FIVE

Pegboard or softboard wall covering

Pegboard is perforated hardboard which can be used to cover sections or complete walls. It not only looks good, retro and funky but provides a really useful storage surface. The holes are used for hooks and pegs for hanging containers, small boxes, speakers and other gizmos. An alternative, useful and inexpensive material is softboard, which is usually used as a liner for school corridor walls. It is very lightweight, and can be stuck onto the wall with panel adhesive and then painted for use as a notice board.

Softboard makes an ideal noticeboard because it is very lightweight, so it can be stuck on the wall with panel adhesive and painted a favourite colour. A few pop-star pin-ups and other teenage collectables will do the rest.

HOW TO DO IT

STEP 1 For the softboard, hold it against the wall and mark the position of the corners. Apply panel adhesive to the back of the softboard and stick it onto the wall. For the pegboard, plug and screw the battens to the wall with hardboard pins.

STEP 2 Hold the moulding up to the wall and mark the position of the mitres. Cut the frame corners with the mitring saw. Drill clearance holes in three places along the length of each side. Mark the screw positions on the walls, and then drill and plug. Apply panel adhesive to the back of the mouldings and screw them to the wall.

STEP 3 Paint the softboard or pegboard to blend in or contrast with the wall colour. Two coats may be necessary for the softboard because it is highly absorbent.

Cabinet Makeovers

Updating your existing furniture is the name of the
decorating game these days, and kitchen cabinets are often the first to
get the makeover treatment, especially if they are dull and made of melamine!
This chapter shows you how easy it is to replace the existing doors on your old
units with new and funky ones, chicken-wire panels or even how to ditch the
doors altogether and use wicker baskets instead. But you don't even have to
go that far – a coat of primer and bright paint makes for a quick and easy
transformation, or you could experiment with different waxes,
washes or other textured finishes.

PROJECT ONE

Replacing existing doors

Achange of doors on the kitchen units is one of the quickest ways to create a new look. Fitted kitchen units are made to a standard size and, although the hinges look quite complex, they are not difficult to fit. Ready-made hardwood doors are widely available and it makes sense to use them if the style is right. The other option is to make them yourself using beech-faced MDF. You get the best of both worlds with a material like this. The MDF backing makes it easy to work with, and the beech facing has all the beauty of the natural grain. You can buy it from good timber merchants in sheets measuring 1.2 x 2.4m/48 x 96in in a 19-mm/¾-in thickness.

Replacing kitchen unit doors is one of the quickest ways to create a new look. Since fitted kitchen units are made to a standard size, you can buy them ready made. Add chrome handles to complete the look.

HOW TO DO IT

STEP 1 Support the door as you unscrew the hinges to remove it. If the screws are in a good condition, save them to re-use in the new door.

STEP 2 If you are making a new door then use the old one as a template to draw around. Check the right-angles and the measurements, and then cut out the new door with a handsaw and sandpaper the edges.

STEP 3 Mark the positions for the hinge fittings, and drill out the recess with the spade bit.

STEP 4 Hold the door in position with the hinge mechanism fitted into the recess, and mark the screw positions. Drill small pilot holes.

STEP 5 Screw the hinges to the doors. The fit of the door can be adjusted using the two screws on the hinge inside the cupboard. Loosen the screws, move the door slightly and re-tighten them. Repeat this sequence until the fit is perfect.

STEP 6 Measure the positions for the screws or bolts accurately. The handles on all the doors must be perfectly aligned, so double check and use a spirit level. Drill holes for the screws or bolts and fit the handles.

PROJECT TWO

Replacing cupboard doors with chicken wire, framed in MDF

This project is suitable for wall-mounted kitchen or base units. If you like the look you could use it throughout the kitchen, but remember that you can see through chicken wire and not everything in a cupboard makes a good display.

Begin by emptying the cupboard and unscrewing the door. Kitchen cupboard hinges tend to leave large holes which will need filling if you are changing the style. Clean the inside of the cupboard with a grease-cutting detergent and paint it a country colour – pale moss green or slate blue, for instance. Melamine will need to be primed first, ideally with an all-surface primer. If you are lining the shelves, do it at this stage before the door is replaced.

Replacing existing cupboard doors with chicken wire suits the country-kitchen look because it puts more of your kitchen on show. It's a good idea to plan the contents of the cupboards before you decide to put them on display.

HOW TO DO IT

STEP 1 Place your outgoing door on top of the MDF. Use it as as a template, drawing the outline onto the MDF. Clamp the MDF on a workbench and wear the mask as you cut it to size, and sand the edges lightly.

STEP 2 Draw the cut-out shape onto the MDF. Drill a hole in one corner of the shape, using an 8-mm/⅝-in drill bit.

STEP 3 Clamp the MDF to the workbench and jigsaw out the inside shape. Keep the jigsaw's foot in touch with the surface of the MDF, and move with the saw.

STEP 4 Use sandpaper to smooth the edge on the inside and outside. Always wear a mask when sanding MDF to prevent you breathing in the fine particles which contain chemicals that are best avoided!

STEP 5 Give the door two coats of primer, following the drying times as directed on the can. Use a foam roller to apply the paint because it will give a better finish than a brush, and painting takes half the time. Apply the top coat in the same way.

STEP 6 Cut the chicken wire to the size of the cut-out shape allowing an extra 25mm/1in all around the edge. Turn over a seam of 10mm/³⁄₈in and flatten it with a hammer. Lay the MDF face down with the chicken wire in position at the back. Staple the panel at the four cardinal points first, then add more staples in between until it is perfectly secure. Re-hang the door.

TIP
• Even with a folded seam chicken wire has sharp pointy edges. As long as the shelves in the cupboard are set back from the door, it is a good idea to cover up these edges with a simple wooden moulding.
• Measure the lengths required, then mitre the corners and use panel pins to secure them.

YOU WILL NEED:
- SCREWDRIVER
- WOOD FILLER
- MOULDING
- MITRING SAW (OR TENON SAW AND MITRING BLOCK)
- MEDIUM-GRADE SANDPAPER
- CONTACT ADHESIVE
- MOULDING PINS
- NAIL PUNCH
- SMALL HAMMER
- ALL-PURPOSE PRIMER
- PAINT (IN A SUITABLE COUNTRY COLOUR)
- SMALL FOAM PAINT ROLLER AND TRAY
- WILLOW BASKETS

PROJECT THREE

Removing cupboard doors and adding willow baskets

Any base unit or kitchen cupboard can be given a real country look by removing the doors, and using willow baskets on the shelves as pull-out drawers. In fact, it may require a leap of the imagination to convert a standard beige melamine cupboard into something beautiful, but it can be done! All you need do is whip off the doors, fill the holes and pop in the baskets, but a few trimmings will make all the difference.

A melamine cupboard can be painted after suitable priming, and the facing edges of the cupboard can be covered with a wooden moulding. They come in a range of styles, from twisted rope and oak leaves to simple half-moon and square edge. The inside of the cupboard will look good painted in a contrasting colour to the outside, and there is also the option of adding a curtain on a simple net wire. Checked gingham or even linen tea towel curtains look a million times better than old melamine, and they can be tied back to reveal the baskets inside.

Willow baskets as sliding, pull-out shelves transform standard melamine cupboards. Paint the insides and outsides of the cupboard first, and add wooden moulding to the facing edges.

HOW TO DO IT

STEP 1 Unscrew the existing doors and remove the fittings. Fill the holes with wood filler so that the filler stands slightly proud of the surface. Once it has dried, sand the filler level.

STEP 2 Measure the frame then cut the moulding to fit, mitring the corners. Apply contact adhesive to the frame.

STEP 3 Stick the moulding down and then add a few pins along each length. Tap the pinheads into the moulding with a nail punch, fill the holes and sand smooth.

STEP 4 Prime the cupboard and then paint it inside and out. If you are using two different colours, paint the inside of the cupboard first and allow it to dry before painting the area where the colours meet.

BASKET HANDLE IDEAS
You can use any of the following...
• Cardboard parcel labels tied on with string
• Checked ribbons
• Stitched tubes of fabric
• Threaded beads or buttons on twists of wire
• Rope loops
• Buckled leather straps

STEP 5 Buy willow baskets to fill the space widthways, leaving just enough room for them to slide easily in and out. Many baskets have handles attached, but if not there are plenty of ways to make your own.

YOU WILL NEED:
- TIMBER: 1 x BACK PIECE NO MORE THAN 300 x 300MM/ 12 x 12IN AND AT LEAST 30MM/1¼IN DEEP; 2 x FRONT PIECES FOR THE DOORS; 4 x SIDES ABOUT 12MM/½IN DEEP AND NO MORE THAN 100MM/4IN WIDE
- 4 HINGES
- 1 IRON BOLT
- SMALL PANEL PINS
- WOOD GLUE
- HAMMER
- SANDPAPER
- HANDSAW
- SCREWDRIVER
- SMALL SCREWS
- BRADAWL
- 6 CUP HOOKS
- 2 MIRROR FIXINGS
- PAINT
- PAINT BRUSHES
- WALL FIXINGS

This Italian-style key cupboard will look great painted in muted Mediterranean colours, with the dappled sunlight falling across it.

PROJECT FOUR

A small shuttered wall cupboard

This shallow cupboard looks like a wooden shuttered window you would find in a farmhouse. On the wall in an entrance hall it creates the illusion of a window, when it is actually a key cupboard. Recycled timber gives the most rustic effect – or use part of a small louvred door.

The idea is to make a box with a decorative lid to hang on the wall. For the backing plate, use timber thick enough to allow for hooks to be screwed in. The traditional colours used for shuttered windows are red-brown or blue-green, both of which soon fade and mellow in the bright sunshine.

TIMBER REQUIREMENTS

back: 290 x 330mm/11½ x 13in;

sides: 2 x 25 x 25mm/1 x 1in, measuring 290mm/11½in;

top/bottom: 2 x 25 x 25mm/1 x 1in, measuring 285mm/11¼in

doors: 140mm x 325mm/5½in x 12½in

panelling: 70mm wide x 290mm long mitred/2¾ x 11½in; 70mm wide x 125mm long mitred/2¾ x 4⅞in

TEMPLATE

Draw a template based on these designs. The cupboard made here is 290 x 330 x 25mm/11½ x 13 x 1in, but adapt your template to the size you require.

HOW TO DO IT

This idea can be adapted to suit your needs or the timber you have available. The cupboard is simply glued and pinned together.

STEP 1 Cut all the pieces to size (see timber requirements, opposite). Sand as necessary.

STEP 2 Make up the shallow box with simple butt joints, using wood glue and panel pins to secure the sides and fix them to the back.

STEP 3 Make up the two front doors, adding extra panels and cross bars to give the shutter style (if required).

STEP 4 Attach the doors to the box base using two hinges for each door.

STEP 5 Fix the iron bolt onto the front to join the doors in the middle.

STEP 6 Apply two coats of paint. When the cupboard is dry, screw six hooks (or more) into the back of it, then fit the mirror fixings onto the back and fix the cupboard onto the wall.

YOU WILL NEED:
- WET AND DRY
  SANDPAPER
- ALL-SURFACE PRIMER
- SMALL FOAM ROLLER
  WITH TRAY
- METHYLATED SPIRIT
  (FOR CLEANING)
- SATINWOOD PAINT
  IN PALE GREEN
  (MAIN COLOUR)
- STENCIL MATERIAL
  (CARD OR PLASTIC)
- CRAFT KNIFE
- TRACING PAPER
  (OR PHOTOCOPIES
  OF PATTERNS)
- MATCH POT OF BRIGHT
  RED (BACKGROUND
  COLOUR)
- MATCH POT OF BLACK
  (FOR THE PATTERN)

PROJECT FIVE

Painting the kitchen units

The idea that melamine kitchen units can be painted is actually quite new. This has a lot to do with TV make-over programmes and the popularity of home style magazines. Once the make-over idea took off people started experimenting, trying different products and discovering new uses for old materials.

The problem with a shiny surface like melamine is that, without the right primer, the paint has nothing to key into and is easily scratched. The trick is to scratch the surface with a wet and dry sandpaper, then apply one or two coats of a shellac-based primer. It gives good coverage, is very strong and leaves an ultra-matt surface.

Go creative on your kitchen units! Melamine kitchen units can be painted as long as they are prepared beforehand, using sandpaper to scratch the surface and primer to give an ultra-matt surface.

HOW TO DO IT

STEP 1 Clean the doors with a grease-cutting detergent or sugar soap. Rub them down with wet and dry sandpaper to remove the shine from the surface.

STEP 2 Apply the primer with the roller and leave to dry (repeat if necessary). Apply the main colour (repeat if necessary).

STEP 3 Enlarge the two stencil patterns and transfer them onto stencil card or plastic. Cut them out with a craft knife. Paint the background shapes first in the light colour. Use the second stencil to apply the pattern inside the shapes, and then apply two coats of clear gloss varnish.

Enlarge the stencils and transfer them onto plastic or stencil paper. The guides to the left will help you position the two main stencils together on your kitchen unit door.

YOU WILL NEED:

- PAINT STRIPPER
- STEEL WOOL
- STRIPPING KNIFE OR SCRAPER
- PAINT BRUSHES
- GLASSPAPER 240 GRIT ALUMINIUM OXIDE
- SCREWDRIVER
- BEADING
- EMULSION
- WOODWASH
- WATER-BASED DYE
- COLOURED WAXES
- VARNISH
- LIMING WAX
- CLEAR WAX
- BRASS FITTINGS
- PATTERNED OR PLAIN GLASS
- PUTTY
- SUGAR SOAP
- GLOVES

PROJECT SIX

Revamping a wooden cupboard

Several different finishes – paint, colourwash, stain, varnish and wax – are used, together with replacement glass and simple brass furniture, to give this well-made but badly neglected cupboard and drawer combination unit a new lease of life.

HOW TO DO IT

STEP 1 The old multi-layered paint finish is removed using a scraper to take off blistered paint after applying water-washable paint stripper. Remember to wear gloves!

STEP 2 When all the paint is removed, steel wool dipped in sugar soap is used to clean the surface thoroughly. Always rub in the direction of the wood grain.

STEP 3 The door is removed and cleaned, and old glass bead and putty discarded. A coat of white emulsion is 'distressed'.

STEP 4 The inside of the cupboard needs to reflect a warm, friendly glow; orange emulsion from a sample pot is ideal.

STEP 5 Diluted woodwash (available in small tins) is painted onto the base and top of the unit. Turquoise was the chosen colour here.

STEP 6 The multi-finish theme continues – diluted ultramarine water-based dye is brushed into the side grain, avoiding the front edge.

STEP 7 The front will remain as bare wood, cleaned up with 240 grit aluminium oxide wrapped around a sanding block.

STEP 8 The waxed drawer is tested to ensure it slides well. Blue and white waxes have been applied and polished.

STEP 9 New brass drawer and cupboard door furniture is fitted to replace the old plastic knobs. Small hands and a stubby screwdriver are needed to gain access to the inside of the drawers.

Hidden Assets

Not everything in your home is worthy of being put
on show, and sometimes it's necessary to hide or disguise certain vital
yet unattractive items. Television and video equipment is a good example:
it does tend to clutter up the living room, so why not hide it behind an
attractively covered screen? Garish videos can also be stowed away in a neat
drawer which is painted to match the skirting board exactly. Kitchen equipment
can also be discreetly hidden, and both a toaster and a food mixer can wear
smart padded covers. Out-of-season clothes – great wardrobe space
devourers – get the same treatment and can be tucked away under
the bed in soft, collapsible cases.

PROJECT ONE

Making a two-panel screen to hide modern equipment

All your efforts to recreate the atmosphere of a traditional sitting room can be ruined by televisions, computers and video recorders. They attract the eye even when they are not switched on. Furniture stores now stock antique reproduction cabinets to conceal high-tech appliances, but they do tend to be expensive and look cheap. If you watch a lot of television it isn't practical to hide it in a cupboard, but you could take it off its stand and put it on something more in keeping with the room's style, such as a tin trunk or a wooden chest. If the room has an alcove, push the equipment back into it, and fit a wide shelf at least 300mm/12in above it. A blind or curtain can be fitted along the shelf edge to conceal everything when not in use. A folding screen is an even easier solution, and it also offers more decorative possibilities.

YOU WILL NEED:

- 25 x 50mm/1 x 2in TIMBER FOR THE FRAMES
- To make a two-panel screen overall size 1500mm high x 750mm wide/60 x 30in, you will need 50 x 25mm/2 x 1in timber for the frames cut into 4 x 1500mm/ 60in and 4 x 375mm/14½in
- 4 SMALL DOOR KNOBS FOR FEET
- MITRING SAW (OR HANDSAW AND MITRING BLOCK)
- TAPE MEASURE
- PENCIL
- WOOD GLUE
- THIN PINS
- SMALL HAMMER
- 3 TWO-WAY HINGES AND SCREWS TO FIT
- BRADAWL
- SCREWDRIVER
- SCREWS
- STAPLE GUN
- WOOD PRIMER AND UNDERCOAT
- PAINT – SATINWOOD OR EGGSHELL FOR A MATT FINISH
- SMALL GLOSS ROLLER AND TRAY

TO FILL EACH FRAME YOU NEED:

- PANEL OF HEAVY UPHOLSTERY FABRIC, TAPESTRY OR IKAT (TIE-DYED) STYLE
- BRAID FOR TRIMMING
- FABRIC ADHESIVE

A folding screen is a portable and decorative way of hiding modern equipment such as computers, televisions and video recorders.

HOW TO DO IT

STEP 1 Apply wood glue to the joining edges and assemble the frames. Screw to fasten. Paint the frames and the moulding with a primer, an undercoat and the final top coat.

STEP 2 Lay the frame over the fabric and cut, leaving at least 38mm/1½in as an overlap.

STEP 3 Stretch the fabric taut and staple it to the back of the frame. Place the first four staples halfway along each side, then staple the corners and several points in between.

STEP 4 Measure the lengths of braid needed to cover the edges. Mitre the corners then apply fabric adhesive to the back edges.

STEP 5 Lay the two screen panels flat, butted up together, and place hinges 100mm/4in from the top and bottom, with one in the middle. Use the bradawl to make small pilot holes for the screws.

STEP 6 Small round feet can be added using brass or wooden cupboard door knobs screwed into the base of the frames.

VARIATIONS
• Fit the sheets of woven
cane in the same way as the fabric.
• Use small screws to secure the fretwork panels to
the frames. You will need to drill clearance holes along
the panel edges, and use a bradawl to make pilot holes
for the screws. Paint the panels to match or
contrast with the frames.

YOU WILL NEED:

- 8 SMALL CASTORS
- LENGTH OF SKIRTING BOARD TO MATCH THE EXISTING ONE (IF IT CAN'T BE RE-USED)
- PANEL ADHESIVE
- 50 x 25-MM/2 x 1-IN BATTEN
- 12-MM/½-IN MDF SHEET FOR SHELF
- 6-MM/¼-IN MDF FOR DRAWER BASE
- 6-MM/¼-IN MDF FOR 4 DRAWER SIDES
- HANDSAW
- THIN PANEL PINS
- SMALL HAMMER
- PAINT AND A BRUSH
- SPIRIT LEVEL
- DRILL
- MASONRY BIT
- WALL PLUGS
- 4-MM/³⁄₁₆-IN DRILL BIT FOR WOOD
- 2-MM/⅛-IN DRILL BIT FOR PILOT HOLES
- SCREWS

PROJECT TWO

Disguised storage

If you really want to disguise something the trick is to make it look the same as everything around it. This project does this by building a boxed-in shelf with a drawer at floor level, and using a skirting-board front to disguise it so well that it could almost be used as a safe. This is also a way to make the most of an alcove by building the shelf wide enough for the TV. If the alcove is not deep enough it will need to be built out at the front, but the basic idea remains the same.

This drawer on castors has been built as part of a low, boxed-in shelf, and disguised with a skirting-board front to blend in with the edges around it.

HOW TO DO IT

STEP 1 Measure the depth of the alcove. If it needs extending, take this into account and cut out 2 side pieces of 25 x 50mm/2 x 1in to support the shelf. If the shelf height is 500mm/19¾in the sides will need to be 488mm/19¼in. Drill and screw to the wall and then check the level.

STEP 2 Cut the shelf to fit the alcove. Cut a U-shaped cable hole on the back edge. Apply a long bead of adhesive to the top edges of the sides and place the shelf on top. Use a hammer to drive in some thin pins to hold the shelf securely. If the alcove is wide, add a supporting leg to the middle.

STEP 3 Make up the two drawers: cut the base of each drawer to fit snugly inside the alcove allowing just enough clearance for it to slide in and out without catching.

STEP 4 Cut drawer sides to match the depth of the shelf, and a front and back to be butted into them.

STEP 5 Fit each of the four castors to the base of the drawer.

STEP 6 Cut the skirting board to fit onto the drawer front (and box sides if the shelf has been built out beyond the alcove). Stick the skirting board onto the drawer front (and box sides if built out) with panel adhesive. Do this so that the skirting board skims the floor, hiding the castors. Paint the sides and front of the drawers to match the walls and the skirting to match the skirting board.

PROJECT THREE

Underbed case

The empty space under the bed is often neglected as a storage area, yet it is ideal for storing spare bed-linen and out-of-season clothing. The items need to be concealed inside containers to protect them from dust: a slim fabric case with a deep gusset can hold many items. You will need two 1000-mm/ 3ft 3-in zips.

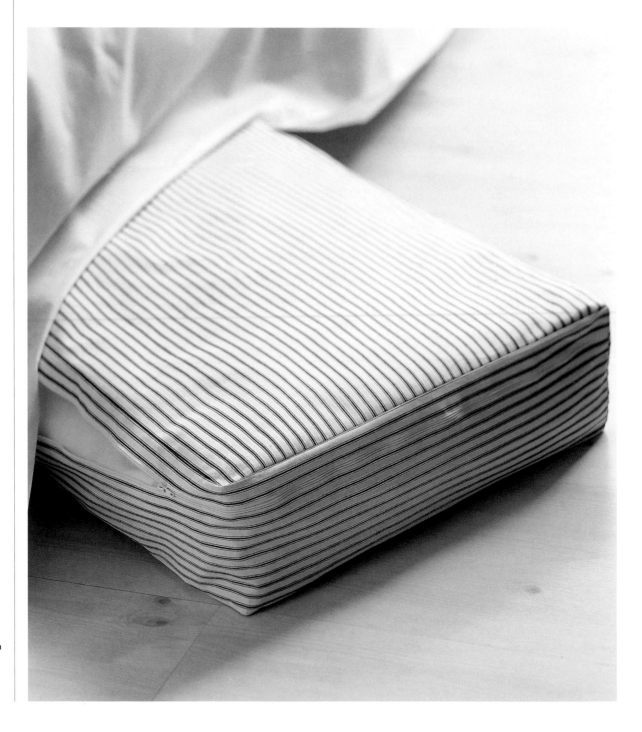

Store out-of-season clothes and bed-linen in a smart, striped, underbed case. This can be stored away unobtrusively.

HOW TO DO IT

STEP 1 Cut a strip of fabric for the base gusset 2000 x 145mm/6ft 6in x 5¾in and a strip of fabric for the lid gusset 2000 x 56mm/6ft 6in x 2¼in. Press 15mm/⅝in under on one long edge of both pieces, and mark the centres of the pressed edges with a pin.

STEP 2 Pin two 1000mm/3ft 3in zips under the pressed edges, with the top ends 10mm/⅜in each side of the centre pins, positioning the pressed edges against the zipper teeth. Zips cut from a continuous length will be unfinished at the top, so open the top of the zips a little and pin the top teeth under the pressed edges so that the zippers do not slip off before stitching. Using a zipper foot, stitch close to each side of the zip.

STEP 3 Cut a strip of fabric for the back gusset 1080 x 178mm/3ft 6¼in x 7in. With the right sides facing, stitch the ends of the zippered gussets to the ends of the back gusset, taking a 10-mm/⅜-in seam allowance, and starting and finishing the seams 10mm/⅜in from the long edges. Neaten the seams with pinking shears or a zigzag stitch. Press towards the back gusset.

STEP 4 Partly unzip the zips to turn right side out. Cut two rectangles of fabric 1080 x 472mm/3ft 6¼in x 18½in for the lid and base. Open out the back seam at the top of the lid gusset. With the right sides facing, pin the back gusset to one long edge of the lid, then continue pinning the lid gusset to the lid. Snip the gusset at the front corners of the lid so the fabric lies smoothly. Stitch in place, taking a 10-mm/⅜-in seam allowance, and pivoting the seam at the corners. Stitch the base gusset to the base in the same way. Neaten the seams with pinking shears or a zigzag stitch. Turn right side out.

YOU WILL NEED:

- FABRIC OF
  YOUR CHOICE
- PATTERN PAPER
- LINING
- WADDING
- PINS
- NEEDLE AND THREAD
- SEWING MACHINE
- TAPE MEASURE
- PENCIL
- AIR-ERASABLE PEN
- CONTRASTING FABRIC
  FOR BINDING
- SCISSORS

PROJECT FOUR

Toaster and food mixer covers

Coordinate your kitchen appliances with a set of matching covers made from light-to-mediumweight fabrics. Here, linen-look fabrics in contemporary designs have a contrasting striped fabric for the lining and binding.

Because toasters and food mixers vary in size, you will need to make your own paper pattern. Measure the height and depth of the machine and add 32mm/1¼in to the measurements. Draw a square or rectangle on paper to these measurements for the end panel. Round off the

top corners by drawing around an upturned glass. Cut out the pattern and check it against the end of the toaster or mixer; it should be at least 10mm/⅜in larger on all sides. Draw the grain line parallel with the side edges.

For the front and back panels, use a tape measure to measure around the sides and top of the end panel pattern, from one corner of the base edge to the other corner of the base edge. Measure the length of the toaster and add 32mm/1¼in to this measurement.

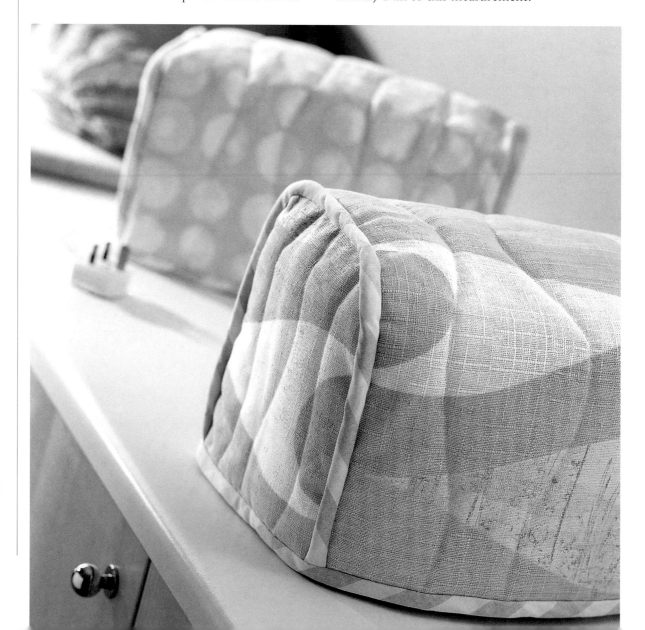

A set of matching appliance covers can look very stylish, especially if you choose fabric that blends in with your colour scheme.

HOW TO DO IT

STEP 1 Use the pattern to cut two end panels from the fabric, the lining and 56g/2oz wadding. Cut one rectangle each of fabric, lining and wadding to the front and back panel measurements. Sandwich the wadding between the fabric and lining, with the right sides facing outwards. Tack the layers together along the outer edges.

STEP 2 Set the sewing machine to a slightly longer stitch length than usual. Starting at the centre of the upper edges, stitch along the length of the panels in random wavy lines about 70mm/2³⁄₄in apart. Draw guidelines with an air-erasable pen first if you prefer.

STEP 3 With the wrong sides facing, pin and tack each end piece to the long edges of the front and back panel, taking a 10-mm/³⁄₈-in seam allowance.

STEP 4 Cut two 83mm/3¹⁄₄in -wide bias strips of contrast fabric the length of the front and back panel, to bind the end seams. Press the bindings lengthwise in half. The binding is applied double: pin each binding to the tacked seam with the right sides of the binding and front and back panel facing. Stitch, taking a 10-mm/³⁄₈-in seam allowance. Turn the pressed edges over the raw edges and slipstitch along the seam on the end panels.

STEP 5 Cut an 83mm/3¹⁄₄in-wide bias strip of contrast fabric the length of the lower edge of the cover plus 25mm/1in. Press the binding lengthwise in half. Pin the binding to the lower edge with the right sides facing. Stitch, taking a 10-mm/³⁄₈-in seam allowance. Turn the pressed edges over the raw edges and slipstitch along the seam inside the cover.

Office Solutions

If you are working from home, then it is vital that you have
a designated work area and that you are as organised as possible –
which means having plenty of places to put paper, pens and pencils, and other
associated office clutter. Children and teenagers also benefit from having a
decent desk at which to study. Cheap desks are easy to get hold of, and can be
customised in the latest acceptable teenage style. Moveable storage is always
useful, and the unit on wheels is large enough for box files and paperwork,
yet small enough for floppy disks and pencils. A free-standing desktop unit
is also described which, in theory, you could move to
wherever you wanted to work.

YOU WILL NEED:
- 1 PLAIN AND VERY CHEAP DESK (SECOND-HAND IS BEST)
- 1 LARGE CAN OF ALUMINIUM PAINT, PLUS SMALL CANS OF OTHER COLOURS (YOU WILL NEED TWO COLOURS FOR EACH NUMBER STENCIL THAT YOU CHOOSE)
- STENCIL CARD
- PENCIL
- SCALPEL
- MASKING TAPE
- SPRAYMOUNT

PROJECT ONE

Customising a cheap computer desk in the hip-hop style

Everyone needs somewhere to work but that doesn't mean it has to look boring and worthy. This project takes a really cheap, white-laminated, fibreboard desk and gives it street cred. The numerals could be exchanged for letters done in the same shadowed style, and whatever pattern you choose, remember it doesn't matter if it's slightly off-centre or if the spray drifts a bit at the edges – it'll still look really good.

A basket-ball style stencil has transformed this cheap, white-laminated fibreboard desk. Add stickers, labels and logos to complete the look.

HOW TO DO IT

STEP 1 Take a photocopy from a favourite sports sweatshirt.

STEP 2 Enlarge the numerals to about 300mm in length and transfer the patterns onto the stencil card. Cut out two stencils. One should just be the letter outline, the other should have stencil bridges added on letters such as Os and Rs to keep the shape intact.

STEP 3 Use a scalpel to cut out the stencils. Spray the back with Spraymount. One stencil is for the main motif, the other for the border.

STEP 4 Protect a well-ventilated area with lots of newspaper and then roller or brush the aluminium paint onto the desk.

STEP 5 Attach the first stencil to the desk with masking tape. Spray this with your first chosen colour.

STEP 6 Spray through the second stencil in the second colour to create the border. Repeat this as many times as you like on the top, the outsides and insides and then add as many stickers, logos and labels as you like.

YOU WILL NEED:
- A SHEET OF
  19-MM/³/₄-IN MDF
  CUT AS FOLLOWS:
  BACK 62 X 89CM/
  24 X 35IN
  TOP SHELF 30 X
  89CM/12 X 35IN
  BOTTOM SHELF 25 X
  30CM/9³/₄ X 12IN
  SMALL SIDE SHELVES
  15 X 15CM/6 X 6IN
  (2 PIECES)
  LEFT-HAND SIDE 62 X
  66CM/24³/₈ X 26IN
  RIGHT-HAND SIDE 62 X
  20CM/24³/₈ X 8IN
  LEFT UPRIGHTS 45 X
  30CM/17⁵/₈ X 12IN
  (2 PIECES)
  RIGHT UPRIGHTS 45 X
  15CM/17⁵/₈ X 6IN
  (2 PIECES)
- No. 6 38-MM/1¹/₂-IN
  SCREWS
- WOOD GLUE
- WORKBENCH
- JIGSAW
- TAPE MEASURE
- COMBINATION
  SQUARE
- CARPENTER'S PENCIL
- DRILL WITH PILOT,
  SCREW AND
  COUNTERSINK BIT
  (USE SIZE NO. 4
  SCREWSINK BIT
  FOR ALL THREE)
- LONG RULER
- SANDPAPER
- SPIRIT LEVEL

When this desktop
unit is put on a table
it creates an instant
work surface. It keeps
all your desktop
clutter in an
organised space,
which can be quickly
put away after use.

PROJECT TWO
Building a desktop unit

The work surface can be a table or simply a sheet of thick board supported on a pair of trestles, but what turns it into an efficient desk are the drawer units, shelves and storage space. This project shows how to build a free-standing unit to sit on top of the work surface. It includes space for the computer monitor, storage for CD-ROMs and discs, two file compartments, a stationery tray compartment and a book-ended shelf on the top.

HOW TO DO IT

STEP 1 Hold the uprights, dividers and shelves against the back section and mark out their positions in pencil on the back.

STEP 2 Draw, cut and sand the mitred corners on the two sides.

STEP 3 Measure and draw a 15-cm/6-in-square box at the bottom of the central section on the back piece. This will be cut out to serve as a channel for the computer cables.

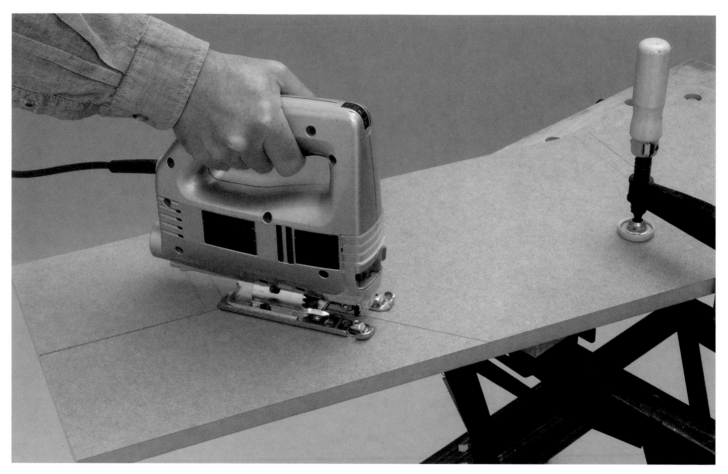

STEP 4 Use a jigsaw to cut out the cable box and the top shelf shape.

STEP 5 Drill clearance holes on the back section and countersink.

STEP 6 Fix the uprights to the back section.

STEP 7 Fix the sides to the two uprights. Fix the smaller shelves to the sides and back.

STEP 8 Fill the holes, sand and paint in your chosen colour.

Use this sketch to help you construct your desk. Remember to measure all the timber accurately and use a spirit level to ensure that everything is level.

PROJECT THREE

Storage

There is no getting away from storage. Whatever type of work you do, paperwork mounts up, records must be kept and we all need somewhere to keep telephone directories and reference material. This storage unit on castors will take care of books, files and catalogues. The top is at desk height, so with a piece of MDF laid on top it provides an extra work surface.

This handy storage unit on castors keeps books, files and catalogues accessible at the same time as neatly stored away. An optional top surface of MDF will make an additional work surface.

HOW TO DO IT

STEP 1 Cut the back of the unit from the sheet of MDF. It should be the height of your desk minus the height of the castors if you want to extend the desk area. Cut out all the shelves, dividers and the top, sides and bottom of the unit.

STEP 2 Draw the positions of the sides, top and bottom, and all the partitions and shelves in pencil on the back. Use a length of MDF to do this so that you can see a flat plan of the unit on the back.

STEP 3 Drill clearance holes to fix all the pieces to the back of the unit. Hold each piece in position as you drill through the clearance holes to make pilot holes for the screws.

STEP 4 Assemble the outer frame first, applying wood glue to the joining edges before screwing them together through the back. Drill pilot, clearance and countersink holes, then secure the corner joints by screwing them together. Fit all the partitions in place first, and then add the shelves. Drill, glue and screw each one so that the whole unit stands firm.

STEP 5 Finally drill holes and fit the four castors onto the base of the unit.

STEP 6 Sand all the sharp edges smooth, then paint if required, or use it just as it is.

YOU WILL NEED:
- 1 SHEET OF
  25-MM/1-IN MDF
- 4 DESK LEGS
  AND FITTINGS
- DRILL
- 2-MM/$^3/_{32}$-IN
  DRILL BIT FOR
  PILOT HOLES
- JIGSAW
- PATTERN
- PENCIL
- 4 SQUARES OF TIMBER
  TO MOUNT THE LEG
  FITTINGS ON
- 4-MM/$^3/_{16}$-IN
  DRILL BIT FOR
  VERTICAL HOLES
- MDF PRIMER OR PVA
- PAINT OR STAIN
- SANDPAPER

PROJECT FOUR
Making a curved desk

Y ou can make a very smart desk from one sheet of MDF and a pair of trestles. Or you can buy the legs in sets of four, as shown in this project, which are then simply attached to the underside of the desk. This desk is ideal for someone whose desk is always piled high because it is shaped like a curve, so when you sit at it, everything is within arm's reach.

A simple curved desk made out of MDF is both stylish and functional. You can either buy a pair of trestles or four, readymade legs.

HOW TO DO IT

STEP 1 Support the MDF between two saw horses or trestles. Draw the curve in pencil, either from the pattern or to your own plan. Cut out the curve with a jigsaw and sand.

STEP 2 Support the desk leg in the work bench and drill a vertical hole for fitting, using the correct drill bit for your screws.

STEP 3 The leg fittings consist of two parts – one post with a screw fitting to fit into the leg and one to receive the post which fits under the table top.

STEP 4 Screw the squares of timber to the underneath of the table, then mark the positions for the legs and all their screws. Drill pilot holes using a 2-mm/³/₃₂-in drill bit.

STEP 5 Screw the top receiving plate of the leg fitting into the timber boss.

STEP 6 Screw each leg into position. Lift the table and turn. Seal the surfaces with MDF primer or a 50:50 dilution of PVA and water. Paint or stain and varnish the desk.

TIP
* These table legs are sold in packs in DIY stores, and always have instructions included with them. If you prefer, you could use trestle table legs, which can also be found in DIY stores.

Soft Options

Fabric storage systems are useful for more delicate items –
such as jewellery and special occasion outfits – and are flexible enough to
also store shoes, bed-linen and children's toys. Drawstring bags make good
receptacles for cosmetics, such as cotton-wool balls and cotton buds, as well as
heavier items, while attractive lined baskets, which can be easily transported
from room to room, are useful for all that new-baby paraphernalia. An entire
wardrobe front can even be constructed from fabric, which can lend a
softer edge to a bedroom, and clothing envelopes and suit covers can
neatly hide away and protect all those excess clothes.

YOU WILL NEED:
- FABRIC OF
  YOUR CHOICE
- THREAD
- SEWING MACHINE
- SCISSORS
- PINKING SHEARS
- STEAM IRON
- PINS
- 2 x 800-MM 31½-IN
  LENGTHS OF CORD
- BODKIN

PROJECT ONE

Drawstring bags

Drawstring bags are fantastically useful, and if you make yourself a set in pretty toning colours, you'll wonder how you managed without them. They make an attractive addition to the bedroom for make-up and jewellery storage and can be used in the bathroom for cotton-wool balls and cotton buds. They are essential for keeping children's rooms tidy too!

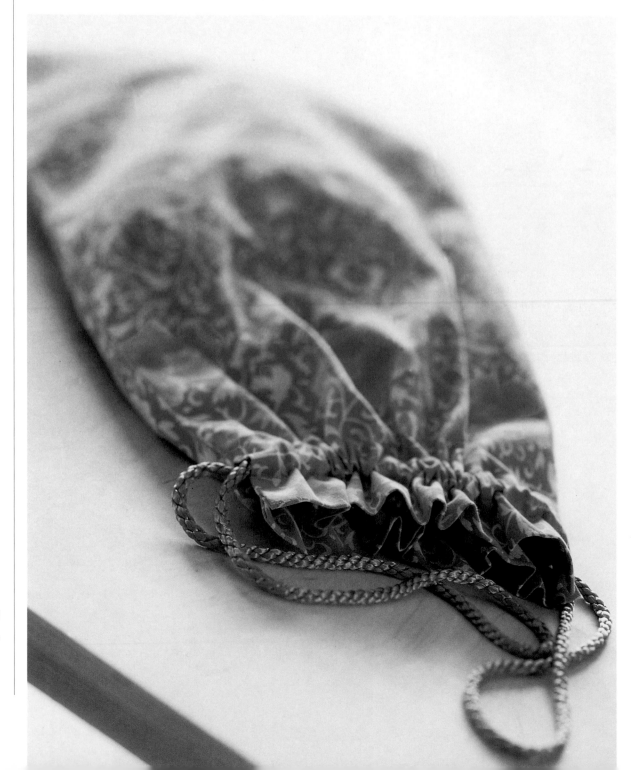

Make this drawstring bag in velvet for precious valuables or a sturdy cotton-lined version with waterproof fabric for use on the beach.

HOW TO DO IT

This medium-size drawstring bag is very
versatile and is a good size for storing footwear or clothing.
Take a 15-mm/⅝-in seam allowance throughout, and
simply change the dimensions of the rectangles to make a
bag that will match your exact requirements.

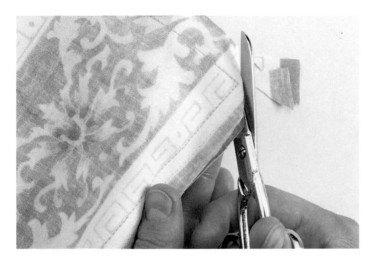

STEP 1 Cut two rectangles of fabric 630 x 380mm/24¾ x 15in. With the right sides facing, stitch the fabrics together along the long side edges and lower short edge, starting and finishing 140mm/5½in below the upper edges. Clip the corners.

STEP 2 Press the seam open, and press the side edges above the seam open. Neaten the seam with pinking shears. Press 15mm/⅝in under then 65mm/2⅝in on the upper edges for the drawstring channels. Pin in place.

STEP 3 Stitch 6mm/¼in above the lower pressed edge then 32mm 1¼in below the upper pressed edge to form the drawstring channels. Turn the bag right side out.

STEP 4 Sew the end of an 800-mm/31½-in length of cord to a bodkin and thread through the channel from the left-hand side of the front channel and out of the right-hand side of the back channel. Repeat with another length of cord through the right-hand side of the front channel, emerging through the left-hand side of the back channel. Knot the cord ends together and adjust them so the knots are hidden in the channels.

PROJECT TWO

Lined baskets

YOU WILL NEED:

- FABRIC OF
  YOUR CHOICE
- WADDING
- NEEDLE AND THREAD
- SEWING MACHINE
- SCISSORS
- PINS
- BODKIN
- STEAM IRON

Baskets come in all shapes and sizes, and a complementary lining adds a nice touch as well as giving protection to the contents. Linings can be attached to the baskets with ties threaded through the weave of the basket or tied around the handles. A lined basket is extremely useful.

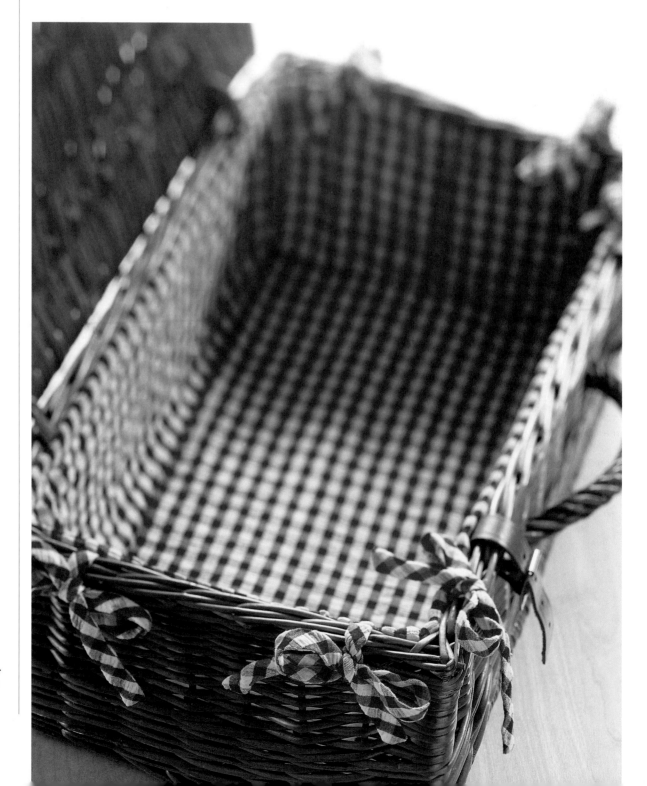

Line a favourite picnic basket with cheerful gingham or line a Moses basket as a present for a newborn baby.

HOW TO DO IT

Choose light-to-mediumweight fabrics, and use a straight-sided basket for best results. This lining for a picnic basket is padded to give some protection to breakables. The tie fastenings can be in a contrasting colour if you wish.

STEP 1 Measure the height of the inside of the basket, then measure the length of the sides at the top of the basket, again on the inside. Cut a strip of fabric for the side panel that is the length of the four sides plus 32mm/1¼in by the height measurement plus 50mm/2in. Cut a strip of 56g/2oz wadding that is the length of the four sides plus 32mm/1¼in by the height measurement plus 15mm/⅝in. Tack the wadding to the side panel 25mm/1in below the upper edge.

STEP 2 Cut one square or rectangle of fabric and 56g/2oz wadding for the base that is the length of one side plus 32mm/1¼ in by the length of an adjacent side plus 32mm/1¼in. Tack the fabric and wadding base together along the outer edges.

STEP 3 With the right sides facing, stitch the short edges of the side panel together, taking a 15-mm/⅝-in seam allowance. Trim away the wadding in the seam allowance. Press the seam open, taking care not to squash the wadding flat. Press 10mm/⅜in under then 25mm/1in on the upper edge. Stitch close to the inner pressed edge.

STEP 4 With the right sides facing, pin the side panel to the base, taking a 15-mm/⅝-in seam allowance and snipping the panel at the corners so the fabric lies flat. Stitch in place, pivoting the seam at the corners. Trim away the wadding in the seam allowance, and neatly clip the corners.

STEP 5 Cut eight bias strips of fabric for ties 460 x 38mm/18 x 1½in. Fold lengthwise in half with the right sides facing and stitch the long edges, taking a 6-mm/¼-in seam allowance. Turn right side out with a bodkin. Turn in the ends and press flat. Slipstitch the ends closed.

STEP 6 Slip the lining into the basket and mark the position of the ties (usually one at each side of the corners). Remove the lining and match the centre of each tie to the stitching line of the hem on the wrong side of the lining at the positions marked. Stitch back and forth a few times across the centre of the tie to attach it securely.

YOU WILL NEED:

- FABRIC OF
  YOUR CHOICE
- PINS
- SEWING MACHINE
- THREAD
- PINKING SHEARS
- PAIR OF COMPASSES
- PAPER
- SCISSORS
- BODKIN
- 2 x 1760-мм/
  5FT 8-IN LENGTHS
  OF CORD
- STEAM IRON

PROJECT THREE
Spare duvet bolster bag

Spare duvets never seem to have a home of their own, and often get packed away uncovered at the top of the airing cupboard, where they can get musty. Sew a simple bolster bag to keep your spare bedding tidy and clean. A set of bags could be made a feature of and hung up on a rail or you could put them in a cupboard or stow them neatly under the spare-room bed.

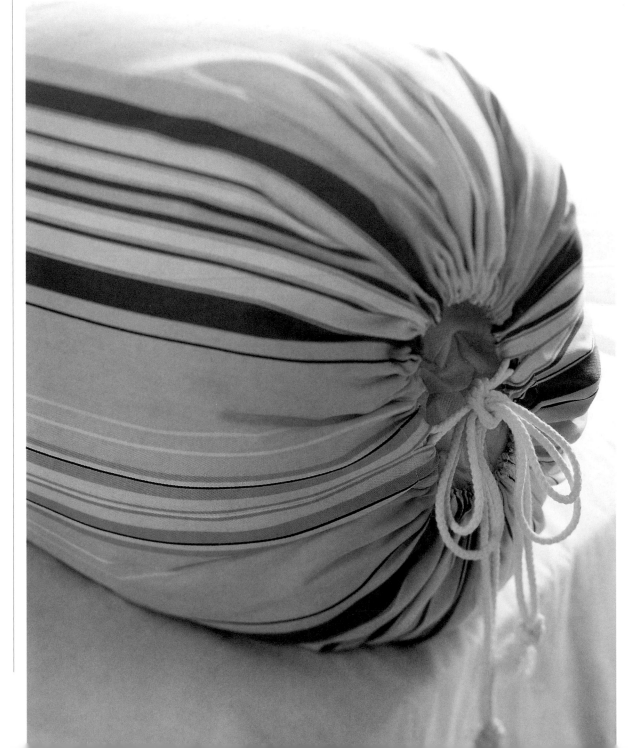

Bolster bags look good made in striped or checked fabric, with a contrasting coloured cord tie.

HOW TO DO IT

Make the bolster bag from light-to-mediumweight fabric, bearing in mind that lightweight fabrics are easier to draw up than thick fabrics. Take 15-mm/⅝-in seam allowances throughout.

STEP 1 Cut two rectangles of fabric for the bolster 1270 x 660mm/4ft 2in x 2ft 2in. Pin the bolsters together along the long edges with the right sides facing, forming a tube. Stitch the side seams, leaving a 25 mm/1-in gap 56mm/2¼in below the upper edge for the drawstring channel.

STEP 2 Press the seams open and neaten them with pinking shears or a zigzag stitch. Press 20mm/³⁄₄in under then 38mm/1¹⁄₂in on the upper edge for the drawstring channel, and pin in place. Stitch close to the upper edge then 25mm below the upper edge to form the channel.

STEP 3 To make a pattern for the base, use a pair of compasses to describe a 430-mm/17-in diameter circle on paper. Cut out the circle to use as a pattern to cut one base from fabric. Fold the base into quarters and snip into the circumference at the folds. Fold the lower edge of the bag in half and snip the fabric at the folds.

STEP 4 With the right sides facing, pin and stitch the base to the bolster, matching the snipped notches and the notches to the seams. Neaten the seam with pinking shears or a zigzag stitch. Turn right side out.

STEP 5 Using a bodkin, thread a 1760-mm/5ft 8-in length of cord through the channel, entering and emerging through the same hole. Knot the ends together, then fray the cord below the knot. Thread another length of cord through the other hole in the same way.

TIP
If you wish to trim the bag with ribbon, stitch one bolster seam first. Stitch ribbons or braid in bands across the piece, then stitch the other seam.

YOU WILL NEED:

• PATTERN PAPER

• SCISSORS

• FABRIC OF
   YOUR CHOICE

• NEEDLE AND THREAD

• SEWING MACHINE

• 1090-MM/43-IN ZIP

• ZIPPER FOOT

• PINS

• STEAM IRON

PROJECT FOUR

Clothes covers (plain)

Clothes covers protect clothing from snagging on other items and keep them clean. Closely-woven natural fabrics keep dust out but allow the clothes to breathe. Plastic-coated fabrics are ideal for covers that are used for travelling, as they will protect against bad weather, but do not to store clothes in them for long periods as the air will not circulate.

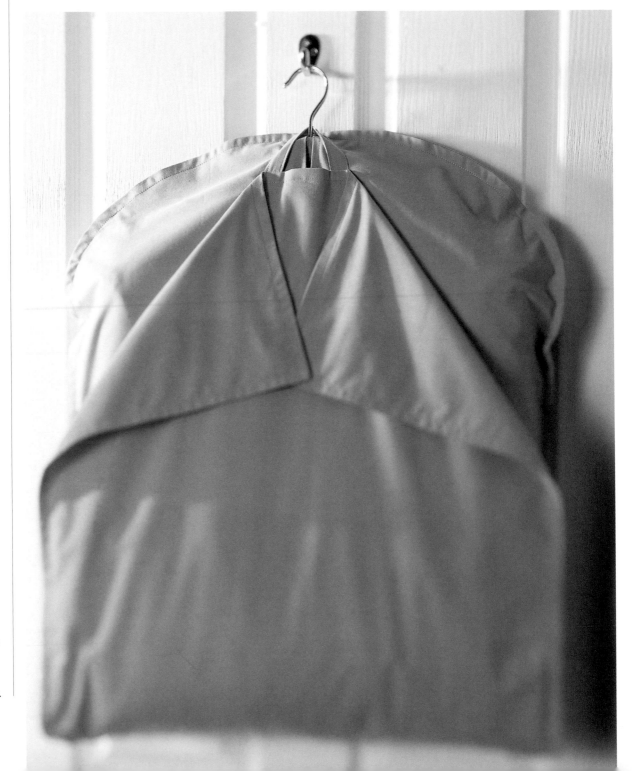

Protect special-occasion outfits with a smart set of clothes covers that can hang neatly at the rear of your wardrobe or on the back of your door.

HOW TO DO IT

STEP 1 Refer to the diagram on page 85 to make a pattern for a cover on paper. Cut out the pattern and use it to cut two fronts and one back (to the fold) from the fabric.

STEP 2 With right sides facing, tack the centre front seam, taking a 15-mm/⅝-in seam allowance. Stitch the seam for 20mm/¾in at the upper end and 178mm/7in at the lower end then press open.

STEP 3 With the front lying face down and starting at the base of the zip, place a 1090-mm/43-in zip face down centrally along the tacked seam. Pin and tack the zip in position. A zip cut from a continuous length will be unfinished at the top so open the top of the zip a little and pin the top teeth under the seam allowances so the zipper does not slip off before stitching.

STEP 4 Using a zipper foot on the sewing machine and with the front right side up, stitch the zip in place 8mm/5⁄16in from the tacked seam and across the base end of the zip. Continue the stitching to the upper edge of the fronts. Remove the tacking stitches.

STEP 5 Cut a strip of fabric 170 x 56mm/6¾ x 2¼in for the hanging loop. Press 10mm/⅜in under along the long edges. Press the strip lengthwise in half and stitch close to both pressed edges. Pin and tack the ends 32mm/1¼in each side of the centre front seam at the lower edge on the right side.

STEP 6 Open the zip. Pin and stitch the front and back together with right sides facing, taking a 10-mm/⅜-in seam allowance. Clip the corners and snip the curves, then turn right side out and press. Topstitch 10mm/⅜in from the outer edges.

YOU WILL NEED:
- **PATTERN PAPER**
- **SCISSORS**
- **FABRIC OF YOUR CHOICE**
- **NEEDLE AND THREAD**
- **SEWING MACHINE**
- **ZIPPER FOOT**
- **965-MM/38-IN ZIP**
- **PINS**
- **PINKING SHEARS**
- **SCISSORS**
- **STEAM IRON**

PROJECT FIVE

Clothes covers (gussetted)

This clothes cover has a generous gusset, making it deep enough to hold a suit or a few lightweight garments. Use a 965-mm/38-in zip that has been cut from a continuous length.

A gussetted clothes cover is ideal for more bulky items, or several items of clothing that you want to store away for a while.

HOW TO DO IT

STEP 1 Refer to the diagram below to make a pattern for a cover on paper. Cut out the pattern and use it to cut two fronts and one back (to the fold) from fabric. With the right sides facing, tack the centre front seam, taking a 15-mm/⅝-in seam allowance. Stitch the seam for 38mm/1½in at each end and press the seam open.

STEP 2 With the front lying face down, place a 965-mm/38-in zip centrally face down along the tacked seam. Pin and tack the zip in position, pinning the top teeth under the seam allowances so the zipper does not slip off before stitching. Using a zipper foot on the sewing machine and with the front right side up, stitch the zip in place 8mm/⁵⁄₁₆in from the tacked seam and across the ends of the zip. Remove the tacking stitches.

STEP 3 Measure the outer edge of one half of the front, 10mm/⅜in in from the raw outer edges. Cut two 83mm/3¼in-wide strips of fabric for the gusset that are the front measurement plus 25mm/1in. With the right sides facing, stitch one end of the gussets together to make one long length, taking a 10mm/⅜in seam allowance. Neaten the seam with pinking shears and press open. Press 6mm/¼in under then 10mm/⅜in on the raw ends, and stitch close to the inner pressed edges.

STEP 4 Pin and stitch the gusset to the front with the right sides facing, with the ends of the gusset meeting end to end at the top of the centre front seam, taking a 10-mm/⅜-in seam allowance. Snip the gusset at the corners so the fabric lies smoothly. Stitch a few times over the top of the centre front seam to reinforce it.

STEP 5 Open the zip, then pin and stitch the gusset to the back in the same way. Clip the corners and neaten the seams with a zigzag stitch or pinking shears. Turn right side out.

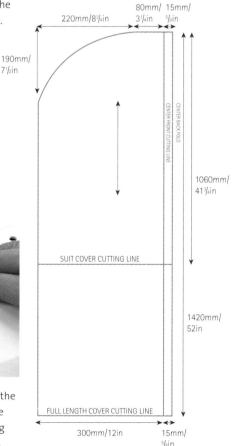

220mm/8¾in · 80mm/3¼in · 15mm/⅝in

190mm/7½in

CENTER BACK FOLD
CENTER FRONT CUTTING LINE

1060mm/41¾in

SUIT COVER CUTTING LINE

1420mm/52in

FULL LENGTH COVER CUTTING LINE

300mm/12in · 15mm/⅝in

YOU WILL NEED:
- FABRIC OF
  YOUR CHOICE
- STEAM IRON
- PINS
- NEEDLE AND THREAD
- SEWING MACHINE
- 510-MM/20-IN
  LENGTH OF
  STRIPWOOD,
  25MM/1IN WIDE AND
  4MM/3¹⁄₁₆IN THICK
- SCISSORS
- 2 EYELETS
- EYELET PLIERS
- 2 HOOKS

PROJECT SIX

Shoe caddy

There is not always enough space to store shoes at the bottom of a wardrobe and a shoe caddy is a practical solution to the problem of freeing up space. It can be hung on a wall or the inside of the wardrobe door. Make the caddy from a hardwearing fabric such as canvas, heavyweight calico or mediumweight denim because shoes are quite heavy.

A sturdy shoe caddy will free up a lot of space at the bottom of your wardrobe and allows you to store your footwear neatly.

| PLEAT | | | PLEAT | | PLEAT | | | PLEAT | | PLEAT | | | PLEAT | | PLEAT | | | PLEAT |

20mm/¾in | 90mm/3½in | 120mm/4¾in | 90mm/3½in | 20mm/¾in | 90mm/3½in | 120mm/4¾in | 90mm/3½in | 20mm/¾in | 90mm/3½in | 120mm/4¾in | 90mm/3½in | 20mm/¾in | 90mm/3½in | 120mm/4¾in | 90mm/3½in | 20mm/¾in

HOW TO DO IT

STEP 1 Cut three pocket strips from fabric 1300 x 270mm/51 x 10⅝in. Press 10mm/⅜in then 15mm/⅝in to the wrong side on the upper raw edges and stitch close to the inner pressed edges. Fold the pleats along the solid lines to meet the broken lines. Pin and tack then press the pleats.

STEP 2 Press 15mm/⅝in to the wrong side on the lower raw edge and tack in place.

STEP 3 Cut a rectangle of fabric 1m x 580mm/39 x 22¾in for the caddy. With right sides uppermost, lay the strips across the front, matching the short raw edges to the long edges of the caddy. Pin the lower strip 20mm/¾in above the lower edge. Pin the middle and top strip with a 60-mm/2⅜-in gap between all the pocket strips.

STEP 4 Tack the side and lower pressed edges of all the strips. Topstitch close to the lower pressed edges of the pocket strips then 5mm/¼in above the first stitching.

STEP 5 To form separate pockets, stitch between the broken lines of the pleats. Stitch back and forth a few times at the top of the stitching to reinforce the seam.

STEP 6 Cut a strip of fabric 580 x 110mm/22¾ x 4¼in for a facing. Press under 15mm/⅝in on the long lower edge. With right sides facing, stitch the facing to the upper edge of the caddy taking a 15-mm/⅝-in seam allowance. Press the facing to the wrong side and topstitch close to the upper edge then 5mm/¼in below the first stitching.

STEP 7 Stitch close to the lower edge of the facing then 40mm/1½in above the lower pressed edge to form a casing. Slip a 510mm/20in-long length of 25mm/1in-wide and 4mm/³⁄₁₆in-thick stripwood into the casing.

STEP 8 To bind the side and lower edge of the caddy, cut two straight 60mm/2¼in-wide strips of fabric 1m/39in long for the side edges and one strip 690mm/24in long for the lower edge. Press under 10mm/⅜in on the long edges of the bindings then press lengthwise in half with the wrong sides facing.

STEP 9 Slip one long edge of the caddy inside a side binding with the lower edges level. Turn under the end of the binding at the upper edge and tack together through all the layers. Repeat on the other side edge. Stitch close to the inner pressed edge of the bindings.

STEP 10 Slip the lower edge of the caddy inside the lower binding with the binding extending at each end. Turn under the ends and tack through all the layers. Stitch close to the inner pressed edge of the binding. Remove the tacking. Lay the batten centrally in the casing. Fix an eyelet 25mm/1in inside each top corner to hang on hooks.

YOU WILL NEED:

• FABRIC OF
  YOUR CHOICE
• SEWING MACHINE
• THREAD
• STEAM IRON
• PINS
• SCISSORS
• 2 BUTTONS
• NEEDLE
• 2 TOUCH-AND-
  FASTEN DISCS

PROJECT SEVEN

Tented wardrobes

Freestanding wooden units are very cheap and are great for storage purposes. The only drawback is that they are usually unattractive to look at and everything in them is on display.

Make a streamlined fabric cover to hide the unit's contents which rolls up and fastens with buttons to give access inside the unit. Fix a clothes rail inside if necessary.

Conceal an unattractive unit behind a fetching fabric cover. This streamlined case fits the shape of the unit exactly.

HOW TO DO IT

Take a 15-mm/⅝-in seam allowance throughout.

STEP 1 Measure the width, depth and height of the unit. For the door, cut two rectangles of fabric the height of the unit minus 40mm/1½in by the width of the unit. With right sides facing, stitch together along the side and lower edges. Clip the corners and turn right side out. Press and pin the upper raw edges together.

STEP 2 Cut two strips of fabric 450 x 120mm/18 x 4¾in for the straps. With right sides facing, fold the straps lengthwise in half and stitch down the long edges and across one end. Clip the corners, turn right side out and press.

STEP 3 Work a buttonhole to fit your buttons 15mm/⅝in from the finished ends. Pin and tack each strap to the upper raw edge of the underside of the door 70mm/2¾in in from the side edges.

STEP 4 Cut two strips of fabric for the pediment that are the unit width plus 30mm/1¼in by 100mm/4in. With right sides facing, pin the upper edge of the door centrally to a long edge of one pediment.

STEP 5 For the front borders, cut two 170mm/6¾in-wide strips of fabric that are the height of the unit minus 20mm/¾in. Press the borders lengthwise in half with the wrong sides facing. Pin and tack the long raw edges together.

STEP 6 Matching the raw edges, pin the short upper edges of the borders to the pediment, overlapping the edges of the door. With right sides facing, tack the remaining pediment on top, sandwiching the door, straps and borders. Stitch the upper edge. Turn the pediment right side out and press. Tack the raw edges of the pediments together. Topstitch the pediment close to the seam then 50mm/¼in from the first stitching.

STEP 7 Cut a rectangle of fabric for the sides and back, which is the height of the unit plus 50mm/2in, by the width and twice the depth plus 30mm/1¼in. Join fabric widths if necessary with a flat felled seam. With right sides facing, stitch the front borders and ends of the pediment to the height edges, starting 15mm/⅝in below the upper edge. Press the seam open and neaten the edges with a zigzag stitch.

STEP 8 Cut a square or rectangle for the roof that measures the width plus 30mm/1¼in by the depth plus 30mm/1¼in. With right sides facing, pin the roof to the upper edge of the unit cover, matching the pediment to the width edges. Stitch, pivoting the fabric at the corners.

STEP 9 Turn right side out and slip the cover over the unit. Pin up a double hem. Remove the cover and sew a touch-and-fasten disc to the lower edge inside the front borders. Glue corresponding discs to the lower edge of the unit. Roll up the door. Sew the buttons to the pediment.

YOU WILL NEED:

• FABRIC OF
  YOUR CHOICE
• TRANSPARENT PLASTIC
• DRINKING GLASS
• SCISSORS
• PINS
• NEEDLE AND THREAD
• 25MM/1IN-WIDE
  READYMADE BIAS
  BINDING
• SEWING MACHINE
• POPPER
• SMALL HAMMER

PROJECT EIGHT

Clothing envelopes

These indispensable clothing envelopes are ideal for storing summer beachwear when it is not in use in the winter, and underwear all year round. You don't have to stick to the dimensions shown here – make the envelopes as big as you need them to be.

Neat plastic-fronted envelopes will keep their contents safe, free of dust and easy to see at a glance. A popper fastening seals the envelope and provides easy access when travelling, or for storing underwear or T-shirts and sweaters in your drawers at home.

Choose plain or woven striped or chequered fabric, as both sides of the fabric will be seen. The edges of the envelopes are bound with readymade bias binding.

Attractive, plastic-fronted envelopes can be used to store out-of-season clothes, or are very useful on holiday to hold swimwear, sarongs and suncream bottles.

HOW TO DO IT

STEP 1 Cut a 410mm/16¼in square of fabric for the back, and a 410 x 305mm/16¼ x 12in rectangle of transparent plastic for the front. Place an upturned glass on a corner of the back and draw around it to make a curved corner. Cut out and repeat on each corner of the back. Pin the front to the back, matching the lower and side edges. Cut the lower front corners to match.

STEP 2 Open out one edge of 25mm/1in-wide bias binding. Turn one end under to start and pin to the outer edges, overlapping the ends. Stitch along the fold line taking a 10-mm/⅜-in seam allowance on the envelope.

STEP 3 Turn the binding to the back, enclosing the raw edges. Tack in place, then topstitch close to the pressed edges of the binding.

STEP 4 Following the manufacturer's instructions, attach a popper centrally to the flap. Slip a few items of clothing inside to judge the position of the corresponding popper. Remove the clothes and attach the popper to the front.

PROJECT NINE

Child's wall tidy

Encourage the children to tidy up with a jolly wall tidy for storing small toys and stationery. There are four generous pleated pockets and three patch pockets for smaller items. It is stiffened with a wooden batten at the top and hangs from hooks on coloured ribbons.

This brightly coloured wall tidy might encourage your children to tidy their rooms! Let them choose the fabric for it.

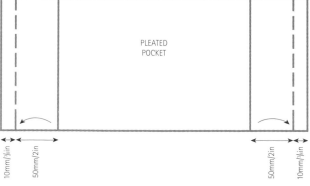

PLEATED
POCKET

10mm/⅜in   50mm/2in   50mm/2in   10mm/⅜in

HOW TO DO IT

Take a 15-mm/⅝-in seam allowance throughout.

STEP 1 From plain fabric, cut two rectangles for the wall tidy 880 x 580mm/34⅝ x 22¾in. Cut four 25mm/1in-wide ribbons 255mm/10in long. Tack the ribbons in pairs to the short upper edge of one wall tidy on the right side, 83mm/3¼in in from the long side edges. With the right sides facing, stitch the wall tidies together, leaving a 200-mm/8-in gap 25mm/1in below the upper edge on one long side edge. Clip the corners, turn through and press.

STEP 2 Cut four rectangles 342 x 260mm/ 13½ x 10¼in from three different fabrics for the pleated pockets. Centre any design motifs. Press 10mm/⅜in then 20mm/¾in to the wrong side on the upper raw edges. Stitch close to the inner pressed edges. Press 15mm/⅝in under on the side edges.

STEP 3 Fold the pleats along the solid lines to meet the broken lines (see diagram opposite). Pin and press the pleats. Press 15mm/⅝in to the wrong side on the lower edge.

STEP 4 Cut three rectangles 195 x 150mm/ 7¾ x 6in from three different fabrics for the patch pockets. Centre any design motifs. Press 10mm/⅜in then 20mm/¾in to the wrong side on the upper raw edges. Stitch close to the inner pressed edges. Press 15mm/⅝in under on the side and lower edges.

STEP 5 Arrange the pockets on the tidy, 38mm/1½in within the side and lower edges and 133mm/5¼in below the upper edge. Topstitch close to the side and lower edges then 6mm/¼in inside the first stitching. Stitch back and forth a few times at the hemmed edge of the pockets to reinforce them.

STEP 6 Stitch across the wall tidy 6mm/¼in then 45mm/1¾in below the upper edge to form a channel. Insert a 32mm/1½in-wide wooden batten 540mm/21¼in long into the channel. Slipstitch the opening closed. Hang the tidy from hooks or a peg rail.

Index